Haunted Heart

A novel

Laverne Stewart

Manor House

Haunted Heart / Laverne Stewart

Library and Archives Canada Cataloguing in Publication

Stewart, Laverne, author

Haunted heart / Laverne Stewart.

ISBN 978-1-988058-30-6 (softcover).

ISBN 978-1-988058-31-3 (hardcover)

    I. Title.

PS8637.T494635H38 2017   C813'.6   C2017-906933-0

Fiction: Novel
Printed and bound in Canada / First Edition.
Front Cover Illustration: Lario Tus / Shutterstock
Interior-layout-edit: Michael Davie
240 pages. All rights reserved.
Published October 2017
Manor House Publishing Inc.
452 Cottingham Crescent, Ancaster, ON, L9G 3V6
www.manor-house.biz / (905) 648-2193
mbdavie@manor-house.biz

"This project has been made possible [in part] by the Government of Canada.
«Ce projet a été rendu possible [en partie] grâce au gouvernement du Canada."

Funded by the Government of Canada
Financé par le gouvernement du Canada

Haunted Heart / Laverne Stewart

Dedicated to my husband and love of my life Robert. As a young couple, early our courtship, we spent a lot of time in Saint John at a Victorian home. I am pretty sure it had a few ghosts of its own including the Loyalist ancestors of the Harrison family who'd owned it until, sadly, it burned to the ground about a decade ago.

I'd like to thank Michael Davie and Manor House Publishing for the great effort he's made to bring my first fiction to print. Thanks to my family for their patience while I was walking the thin line that divides fantasy from reality. Thanks also to readers who encourage me to keep writing.

Haunted Heart / Laverne Stewart

Foreword:

Sarah Harrison, a young Canadian waitress at an upscale Boston restaurant, inherits a mansion in Saint John, New Brunswick.

She heads north to Canada with thoughts of liquidating her estate and returning to her life in Boston.

But things don't quite go as planned.

Sarah finds herself drawn into a new life in the haunted old house she once visited as a young child.

Her new life includes long-time servant Hannah, a sharp-tongued elderly Irish-Canadian woman who converses with spirits of the dead.

There's also Patrick Ryan Gallagher, the handsome contractor with more on his mind than restoring the rundown mansion to its former glory.

Patrick and Sarah embark on a summer fling that seems to be much more than that and is going in a direction neither anticipated. Can they end it before someone gets hurt – or is it somehow their destiny?

And, is it just the old woman Hannah's imagination, or is she actually receiving messages from beyond the graves of ghostly ancestors of the young lovers, ancesters whose own love affair ended in tragedy. Their spirits appear in dreams, late at night, and as bedroom apparitions with disturbing thoughts to share.

Haunted Heart / Laverne Stewart

In addition to all of this, is the menacing rapist Murphy and the ever watchful eyes of hallway portraits.

All of this is much more than Sarah bargained for when she made her fateful trip north to Canada.

Sarah wants nothing more than to sell off the estate and move back to Boston and away from the ghostly confusion – and her growng passion for Patrick.

Sometimes, it seems, a love affair that was meant to be can somehow be ended by judgemental parents and tragic circumstances. Such is the case with with Patrick Gallagher and Sarah Harrison's long-dead ancestors Evelyn Elizabeth Harris and Padraig Gallagher, whose own love affair ended with their sudden deaths. Can they really be reaching out from the Afterlife to guide Sarah and Patrick into a loving relationship and marital union they themselves were denied?

This is a superbly written, intriguing and engaging first novel by accomplished writer Laverne Stewart, bestselling author of non-fiction books **Healing After Homicide** and **Angels and the Afterlife**. It's a ghostly mystery-romance that held my interest from start to finish.

Laverne Stewart has crafted a first–rate novel of the spirit world manipulating the current 'real' world, a novel exploring the tragic love affair of an age-old romance and its impact on the modern-day affair of two star-crossed lovers – highly recommended – a must read!

- **Michael B. Davie,** author, *The Late Man*

Haunted Heart / Laverne Stewart

Praise for Haunted Heart:

When I began reading Haunted Heart I knew right away I was going to love it! Laverne Stewart weaves her stories in a way that brings them to life and attaches them to the reader – heart and soul.

Knowing the other side as I do, and how persistent Spirit can be, this book highlights an incredible story of love that withstands every mortal test in its path.

The main character of Sarah Harrison is especially endearing. After losing her loving father and then a mother who doesn't know how to love, Sarah begins a journey that is more than just inheriting a home from an aged quirky cousin, it's a journey of understanding that love is timeless, and love that is meant to be will endure all that life can throw at it.

Guided by the wisdom and humour of Hannah Sullivan, Irish housekeeper extraordinaire, colourful insightful tours of New Brunswick landmarks and icons, Stewart captures the essence of love through the ages East Coast style; an incredible story of timeless attraction.

- **Suzanne Riley**, Psychic Medium

Haunted Heart / Laverne Stewart

More Praise for Haunted Heart:

Haunted Heart is a book for everyone. It's easy to read and the storyline flows well. It is funny at times but not comical. It is a love story which will make you smile while you try to foresee what's coming right until the end.

There are a few surprises that are both unexpected and delightful. All the characters are enjoyable but two favourites are Chaz and Hannah. Chaz is a good friend to Sarah. He is flamboyant and yet very practical and nonsensical.

Hannah is entertaining with her no- nonsense dialogue. She believes in spirits and is in cahoots with Sarah's long-dead ancestors to bring a romance to fruition.

- **Patricia Anne McKay,** book reviewer and literary editor.

1

Sarah Harrison was exhausted. What she needed after an eight-hour drive from Boston to Saint John was a meal, a bath and some sleep and in that order. She'd just come from a lawyer's office in Saint John where she'd picked up the keys to a home on this unfamiliar city's north end.

As she got out of her Mustang convertible, she stood on the sidewalk in front of the massive property she'd just inherited from an elderly cousin she hardly knew. Sarah was the spinster-lady's only living relative and, because it was important to Gertrude Harrison that the home and its contents remain in the family, all of it came to her.

Sarah looked at the Victorian mansion on Douglas Avenue located in what once was an affluent neighborhood where rich sea captains and other well-to-do gentry lived.

Now, after years of neglect, the house looked as though it needed more than the hedges trimmed and the windows washed to bring it back to its former glory.

Sarah walked up to the massive oak doors, put the key in the lock and turned it until she heard a click. She placed her hand on the doorknob and gave it a twist and pushed it opened. The foyer was almost as large as her apartment. The floor was covered in a marble mosaic that she recognized as the Harrison's family crest. Memories of this place came back to her from when she used to visit here with her parents 20 years earlier.

Sarah remembered the sticky hard candy that old, fussy Gertrude insisted that she take a piece of. She could still feel her mother's sharp fingernail poking her in the back, pushing her forward to take the offering. She put it in her mouth, smiled and murmured 'Thank you cousin Gertrude'. But the minute the adults' attention was off her she would spit the awful mint into a tissue and stick it into the pocket of her dress.

Sarah came back to the present when she felt something brush against her legs. She jumped back and then looked down. It was a very large orange cat with huge paws and a long luxurious tail. She bent down and gave the cat a scratch behind the ears. From the lawyer's letter she'd received at her home in Boston she knew this was Marmalade. Cousin Gertrude had died suddenly a month earlier and ever since, the cat had been taken care of by a caretaker of the property hired by the old woman's lawyer to watch over the place until she was able to arrive and take possession.

"Well Marmalade that was a nice welcome. You were so quiet I didn't hear you. Next time make some noise would you so you don't scare me to half to death?"

With that the cat let out a loud meow and ran as fast as she could out of the foyer and down the hall. From what Sarah could remember of the place, the hall led to the dining room and kitchen. Just then Sarah heard her stomach growling. She hadn't eaten since she was in Portland and that was five hours earlier. She followed the cat down the hall. On the walls oil paintings of ancestors were hung. The stern faces of these great, great, great grandparents used to frighten her when she was a child because she was certain they were casting disapproving looks her way. She was sure their eyes followed her as she ran down the hall. She still felt their eyes on her now.

"Okay," Sarah said firmly, "I'm the lady of the manor now so all of you are put on notice as I am no longer afraid of you!" Despite this show of bravado, Sarah found herself walking quickly past the portraits and felt their eyes were on her. She opened a set of large mahogany French doors and found herself in the dining room. It was just as she remembered it. A large antique dining table with seating for 12 was positioned in the middle of the room. Built-in china cabinets held Wedgwood china and fine crystal goblets.

Sarah walked over to a buffet and pulled open a drawer. It was filled with crisp white linen table linens. Everywhere she looked there was evidence of wealth. She imagined the faces in the hall would have sat at this table and been served gourmet meals by servants.

Once again she heard her stomach growl. She pushed open the heavy wooden swinging door that separated the dining room from the kitchen and walked through the opening. The lawyer had told her the building's caretaker had been told to stock the refrigerator. She opened its door and looked inside. Fruit, cheese, juice, milk, and other perishables filled the shelves. In the pantry she found it fully stocked. She wondered if the caretaker thought a very large family was moving in. Marmalade silently approached and rubbed against her legs causing her to jump once more.

"I thought I made myself clear cat. You really need to stop doing that!"

"Meow!"

"Ok I know you're hungry too. Let's see what's for supper."

She opened a tin of gourmet cat food and emptied its contents into a cat dish she then placed on the floor.

Marmalade ran toward the dish and wasted no time devouring the entire serving. Sarah opened a bottle of water and took a long drink. Next, she made a sandwich from deli meat and cheeses. After she was finished eating she decided it was likely a good idea to get her suitcases from the car and bring them inside. The two bags were heavy. She needed to place them down several times before she managed to get them inside and up the long, winding staircase that led to the mansion's third floor. She had stayed overnight in this place a few times. As a child she was afraid of the sounds. Her father tried to reassure her that it was only the sound of creaking floors and the wind but in her child's mind she was sure this place was haunted.

"Sarah! Don't be so foolish!" her mother used to chastise. "You know perfectly well there are no such things as ghosts or haunted houses!"

"That's right mom. There are no such things as haunted houses or ghosts," she repeated aloud as she continued to pull the heavy bags up the stairs.

Sarah suddenly felt very lonely. She was used to this feeling. Her parents had been in their early 40's when she was born. She was an unexpected surprise to a pre-menopausal mother whom she was sure never really wanted her.

Her mother had a passion for shopping. Sarah had everything any little girl could ever wish for except her mother's time and attention. As a result, she spent much of her time on her own, playing alone in her room. Her companions were her dolls and teddy bears. In her childhood world she was surrounded by friends others couldn't see. They accepted her exactly as she was. These kind and gentle beings were filled with joy and love. Often her mother would hear her talking to them. She would scold her and tell her not to be so foolish. "People will think you're crazy Sarah. Smarten up!"

Sarah learned early in life never to go to her mother for comfort or consolation. Her mother was a self-absorbed narcissist whose main concern was satisfying her own desires. Never could Sarah share a confidence with this woman for whenever she told her mother a secret, it was tucked away in her mother's memory to be later pulled out and used against her in some way. Sarah never felt as though she measured up to her mother's expectations.

Her mother had always been a stranger to her. She couldn't understand her behavior. On the surface the family looked like the model of perfection. Their home was always spotless. Her mother always dressed in the finest clothes. Her hair and make-up were flawless. She loved to entertain. Whenever they were with others she presented herself as the perfect wife and mother. Company often commented on what a wonderful hostess she was. But when the company had gone home and the doors and windows were shut to the outside world, the thin veneer of perfection was stripped back to reveal a very angry woman who hated her life and made Sarah and her father suffer for it.

When Olivia Prescott-Harrison was truly at her worst, she would hurl insults that cut deep. Sarah often thought she would have preferred a slap to the face or have been beaten with a belt rather than to be emotionally sliced apart by her mother's cold and cruel tongue. Her father, also a victim, was paralyzed by co-dependant behavior and gave in to his wife's every demand in the hope that it would stave off another tongue lashing. Her father, although kind, always deferred to his wife's authority, and never intervened whenever her mother decided she needed to be punished for some transgression.

Haunted Heart / Laverne Stewart

When she was a teen her father died suddenly from a heart attack. The emotional and verbal abuses she experienced from her mother worsened. Sarah always thought he'd died from a broken heart due to the emotional pain he suffered throughout their 30 year marriage.

For as long as Sarah could remember she had begged her father to leave her mother. But her dad would simply smile a sad little smile and pat her on the hand and reassure her that it wasn't all that bad. "When she is in a good mood there isn't anything she wouldn't do for us. She loves you Sarah. She just has a hard time showing it," he would tell her when she was younger.

When Sarah was 15 she asked her father why he never filed for divorce. Duncan Harrison was a weak man. He didn't have the courage to stand up for himself and his daughter and face the monster that he'd married. He'd convinced himself there was no chance that a divorce court judge would grant him full custody. He fooled himself into thinking that he stayed in the miserable marriage for the sake of his daughter, who he felt surely would have been abused worse if he'd left the marriage and Sarah remained in the care of his wife.

Sarah remembered the last words her father said to her as he lay dying on the bathroom floor. "I am sorry Sarah. I should have taken you away from her. I should have protected you from her. Now you go and make a life for yourself. You are a strong girl; stronger than me. Leave her Sarah. I love you sweetheart."

He died in her arms just as her mother arrived home from an all-day shopping excursion. "I'm home," she said in a happy sing-song way. She was always happiest when she was shopping.

"Mom! Come quick. It's dad. Help!"

Her mother entered the bathroom and looked down at her husband's body. She screamed and fell to her knees and tore his body from Sarah's arms. "What did you do to him? Call nine-one-one!"

He'd died instantly, the coroner said, as his body was loaded on a stretcher and carried out of their house by ambulance attendants. Sarah cried for him. She cried for herself. She cried for the miserable life they'd both had in this house with that woman. She cried until there were no tears left.

As soon as she could, following high school graduation, Sarah moved out of the family's home and into a bachelor apartment. She went to a community college which she paid for on her own from the minimum wage pay and tips she earned waiting tables in an upscale Boston eatery. Her mother swore when Sarah moved out that she would receive not a dime from her. Her mother was true to her word: Sarah did not receive anything and she didn't want it either. She was determined to live her life on her terms.

Last spring she received a call from a nurse at Tuft's Medical Center advising her that her mother had been admitted and that she was asking for her. It had been three years since she and her mother had spoken. When she walked into her mother's hospital room she was shocked by the sight of the frail, gray-haired woman in the bed on the palliative care unit. For the first time in her life Olivia Prescott-Harrison didn't seem to be the cold and aloof woman she had always been. Perhaps it was the knowledge that she didn't have too many days left and she wanted to make up for past wrongs she had done. They talked for hours. She asked her daughter to forgive her for all of the wrongs she had done in the past. But most importantly she told her she loved her and she apologized for her inability to demonstrate it throughout their relationship. Olivia

Haunted Heart / Laverne Stewart

Prescott-Harrison came from a home where emotions were to be kept to oneself and children were best seen and not heard. Sarah came to realize in their final days together that her mother simply couldn't give her what she had never received from her own parents.

Olivia Prescott-Harrison slipped into a coma and died two days later. The funeral was small and dignified just as her mother had prearranged. After it was over Sarah returned to work at the restaurant and taking part-time university courses. She could have quit her job thanks to the very large inheritance she received from her mother. By now she was used to her life exactly as it was and the others at the restaurant where she worked had become her adopted family so she didn't want to leave them. With the death of Gertrude Harrison, she was an even wealthier 25-year-old.

Sarah decided that because she had no connection to Harrison House or the city where it was located, she would do all of the necessary repairs on this mansion and sell it along with all of its contents.

There were six large bedrooms on the third floor. All of them were filled with hand-carved four-poster beds, dressers and other pieces. The walls were covered in paper which desperately needed to be stripped before they were re-plastered and painted. This was going to be a massive undertaking to prepare this place for sale. While she could do some things on her own, she would need someone far more skilled to do the major restoration work. She made a mental note to call the lawyer's office in the morning and ask for the names of local contractors that specialized in Victorian home restoration.

She walked toward the large windows and pushed back the heavy silk drapes. It was starting to get dark. She felt tired and dirty.

"First a hot bath and then bed," she said to herself. She walked to the nearby bathroom where she saw a large, cast-iron claw-foot soaker tub. She turned on the taps and stuck her wrist under the water to check the temperature. As it filled she went to her suitcases and found her nightgown and cosmetic bag. Inside it there was a travel-size bottle of bubble bath which she poured into running water. She stripped off, stepped into the water and eased her body down into the suds.

"Ah! This is heavenly," she said with her eyes closed. Marmalade had silently snuck up on her again and perched on the edge of the tub near her face. When she opened her eyes she saw the cat staring down at her as it pawed at the bubbles. Sarah screamed. "Look you stupid cat; if you and I are going to get along you need to start listening. I said STOP SNEAKING UP ON ME!"

Sarah cupped the soapy water in her palm and threw it in the cat's direction.

"Meow!"

Marmalade quickly jumped from the tub's edge and managed to avoid getting wet before she scurried from the bathroom for parts elsewhere in the massive structure. As Sarah soaked in silence her imagination got the better of her. This place was creepy. She hated the thought of being the only person here and having to spend the night all alone. Just then she heard a creaky sound. It was the same noise she used to hear as a child.

"It's just the sound of the wind or the building settling," she said aloud to reassure herself. "There's absolutely nothing to be afraid of. The doors are all locked and I am absolutely fine. There are no such things as haunted houses or ghosts!"

After half-an-hour the water was lukewarm and her fingers were wrinkled. She climbed from the tub and wrapped a towel around herself. When she was dried off she slipped on her night gown and robe and returned to the bedroom. Sarah checked her watch. It was now 11 p.m. and she was dead-tired. She pulled the quilt down. She could tell that the bed had been changed with fresh linen for her arrival. She would have to remember to thank the caretaker for all the thoughtful things she had done to prepare for her arrival. She climbed into the massive four-poster bed and pulled the linens over her body. They smelled of lavender. Lovely, she thought as she turned out the light and closed her eyes. She was asleep in a matter of minutes.

Sarah was dreaming. She was standing on a balcony of the mansion looking down on the street. She paced back and forth. It was as though she was waiting for something or someone. Then she went back inside and stared at herself in a mirror. The reflection was her own and yet different. She was wearing a long white gown with an emerald green satin sash that matched the color of her eyes. Her lips were full and red. Her short coppery curls were now long and they cascaded down her back. She looked so sad and lost. Tears streamed down her cheeks as she sobbed. Then Sarah saw herself walking down the curved staircase to the first floor and into the parlor. She saw herself standing in front of a painting. There were tears running down the face on the canvas. The mouth opened and said 'Help me Sarah!' Then the crying turned to screaming but the screams were coming from her mouth rather than the one in the painting.

2

Sarah woke up in a sweat. Confused and afraid, she wasn't sure where she was in the darkened room. She rubbed her eyes and looked at the clock. It was 3:30 a.m.

"What the hell was that?" She got out of bed and went to the bathroom. When she looked in the mirror she saw that her face was wet. She had really been crying in her sleep. She splashed cold water on her face and then dried it with a hand towel.

"Wow I guess that sandwich didn't sit too well. When will I learn not to eat before bed?" she said to Marmalade who hadn't managed to sneak up on her this time and was busily licking its furry belly when the rhetorical question was posed.

Sarah went back to bed but was unable to sleep. After thirty minutes she got up, pulled on her bathrobe and decided that since she couldn't sleep she would try to read. But her mind couldn't stay focused on the book in her hands. She got back out of bed and made her way to the kitchen. She looked in the pantry and found some herbal tea. The box said Sleepy Time. "Perfect," she said to herself as she pulled it from the cupboard and found the kettle to boil some water. When it was ready she poured the boiling water into a mug and placed a tea bag in it. Within a few minutes the tea had steeped. She removed the bag with a spoon and took a sip. The tea-infused hot water had an unusual and yet pleasant flavor.

Sarah allowed her mind to wander as she drank the tea. She looked around the kitchen. This had been a pleasant place to be when she was a kid visiting here with her parents. The housekeeper, she remembered, had been a tiny Irish lady who made the best strawberry jam and scones she had ever eaten. Sarah couldn't remember the woman's face or her name but she recalled that she was full of energy and had made her feel welcome in this kitchen when she didn't feel welcome by Cousin Gertrude or her parents in the other rooms of this house.

Sarah looked at the clock. It was 5 a.m. and the Sleepy Time tea had managed to live up to its name. She yawned and thought that she would have no trouble getting a few more hours of shut-eye. Back through the hallway she went, careful to avoid looking at the stern faces in the portraits that seemed to stare disapprovingly at her. She climbed the stairs and returned to her bedroom where she found Marmalade curled into a tight ball on the other side of the bed.

"Exactly what do you think you are doing cat?"

Marmalade looked up at her innocently as if to say "Who me?"

"Okay, you can stay but stick to your side. Do you hear me?" With that she gave Marmalade a scratch beneath the chin which caused the large orange cat to purr very loudly. "Keep it down will you? I am trying to go back to sleep."

Sarah shut off the lamp on her beside table and closed her eyes. Within a few minutes she was into a very deep sleep. She hardly moved for the next four hours. When she woke she could hear someone downstairs. At first she was afraid it might be someone breaking in but as she became more fully awake and looked at the clock she remembered that the caretaker still had a key and had likely arrived to do some chores. Sarah showered and then slipped on a T-shirt and leggings and went downstairs to find where the sound was coming from. Whoever it was they were in the kitchen.

A tiny, old woman stood at the kitchen sink with her arms up to her elbows in sudsy water. She turned and smiled at Sarah which caused her wrinkled face to become more so.

"Well just look at you! My, aren't you after getting to be a tall, beautiful young woman. I always knew the rest of you would catch up to those long legs of yours."

Sarah stood there for a moment not sure what to say. It wasn't until the lady took a glass jar filled with strawberry jam and a loaf of homemade bread and set them on the table that Sarah realized who it was.

"I remember you. You're...you're..."

"Oh now don't tell me you've forgotten my name girl?! Well never mind. If it's one thing I'm not and that's too full of me self to worry about you not remembering who I am. Well I certainly remember you Sarah Harrison. Why, you were just a wee girl the last time you were here. Well let me refresh your memory girlie; my name is Ahanna Sullivan but most people just call me Hannah. I'm the one who kept you supplied with gingersnap cookies when you were a wee thing. Well now you must be hungry. I thought I'd drop in and cook you breakfast before you started your day. I thought you'd sleep the day away. Here it is almost 9:30 and I've been waiting for you for nearly two hours. You just sit there and I will pour you a nice cup of coffee and make you a bowl of porridge."

"Don't bother. A cup of coffee will be just fine."

"Nonsense girl. You need something to stick to your ribs with the busy day I expect you'll be having. And just look at you. Why I'd swear you'd been living in a refugee camp you are so thin. Well you just let old Hannah feed you and we'll have some curves on you in no time. That's what the men like you know; not these poor things that look like a stiff breeze could knock them on their arses at any minute."

"Really, Hannah, you don't have to go to any trouble. I'll just have the coff…"

"Nonsense. Except for the past month, since Gerti died, Lord be with her, I have cooked breakfast in this kitchen every morning for the last 50 years and I am not about to stop now. No girlie. I am a part of this house just like the floors and walls. The only way you are going to get me to leave here is in a pine box. Now remind me girlie, do you like brown or white sugar on your porridge?"

"Brown," Sarah said realizing there was no point in arguing with this feisty, old Irish lady.

She was glad she consented to eat breakfast. It was sweet and creamy and delicious. When her bowl was empty she asked if there was enough left for a second serving. As Hannah filled her bowl once more she smiled to herself with pleasure. There was nothing Hannah loved any more than seeing people eat her food.

"So tell me now Sarah, how was your first night here at Harrison House?"

"It was okay. It usually takes me a couple of nights in a new bed to get used to it. I woke up early this morning after I had a weird dream and I had to make some herbal tea to help get back to sleep."

Hannah turned her attention from washing the dishes to listen closer to what Sarah was saying. "Do you remember the dream?"

Haunted Heart / Laverne Stewart

Sarah told her that she woke up crying and that in the dream it was a summer night and that she had been very distraught as she paced on the balcony of her bedroom. She described the long white gown with its green satin sash she was wearing along with long white gloves and a green bonnet that was tied with a white bow under her chin. "It was me but why would I dream that I was wearing those old-fashioned clothes and what was I so upset about?"

Hannah wiped her hands in a dishtowel and then put her hands on her hips. "Well it seems you had a visitor last night."

"A visitor? What do you mean?"

"Come with me girlie. It's time you got to know your ancestors."

Hannah led the way down the hall and into the front parlor. On the far wall, above the table grand piano, there was an oil painting. It was an image that Sarah knew well. She was looking at a picture of herself. She studied the image for a while and then looked at Hannah and said "This is crazy. I've never had an oil portrait done of myself."

"That's right. That lady isn't you. It's Evelyn Elizabeth Harrison. And you, girlie, had a visit from her last night."

"What do you mean a visit? I was all alone here last night."

"None of us are truly alone. Those who came before us always watch over us from heaven. Sometimes they like to drop in to say hello from time to time and sometimes, after someone passes, they cannot cross over to the other side because something remains unfinished here that they want or need. I believe the spirit of Evelyn Elizabeth Harrison called on you last night."

Haunted Heart / Laverne Stewart

Sarah stared at Hannah, then turned back to the painting. She didn't want to upset the older woman so she decided not to argue with her. "You mean she visited me in my dreams?"

"Sure she did girlie. Spirits come to us in whichever way they can that they think we will accept. You see, it takes a lot of energy for a spirit to be seen as they were in life. How do you think you would have handled seeing her sitting on the edge of your bed in the middle of the night wanting to have a conversation with you? You would have been scared to death darlin'. Most people can accept what happens in dreams, so that's how the other side tries to get in touch with us."

Sarah stared at the painting. Evelyn Harrison really did look very much like her, she had to agree. But that was all she was prepared to concede to. She had *not* been visited by the spirit of her dead ancestor. That was nonsense. "Have you been visited by her?"

Hannah smiled and nodded. "Oh my word yes dearie; many times. She and I are good friends. I first met her not long after I came to work for the Harrisons in 1967."

"Have you had dreams about her?"

Hannah looked at the portrait and then back at Sarah. "At first; then I would hear her and once in a while I would see her. I remember the first time she appeared to me, I was cleaning the rug in the hallway. I was down on my knees with a scrub brush trying to get out a nasty little stain one of the cats had made. When I looked up there she was. She was just standing there watching me. She was dressed in that same long white gown with the green satin sash you saw in your dreams. She had the saddest expression on her face I'd ever seen in me whole life. In the blink of an eye she was gone. Sometimes I will hear doors slamming.

Haunted Heart / Laverne Stewart

Often I will hear the sound of a lady crying. I know it is her. But don't worry dear. She won't do you any harm."

Clearly this old lady was suffering from dementia or some other form of mental illness. Everyone knows that ghosts are just the stuff of tales to be told around a campfire. Sarah thought it best not to get into a debate about how silly it was to think about spirits and haunted houses, so she decided to continue to play along.

"Well I won't bother her if she doesn't bother me. Hannah; I have decided to hire a contractor to do some work on the house. Don't get me wrong you have done an excellent job. The inside is very clean. But there are things that need to be replaced and restored. The siding needs to be painted and the roof looks like it needs new shingles. I thought I'd have a contractor go through the place and give me an estimate. Do you know contractors in the area I could call?"

Hannah loved this old home as much as if it was her own. She hated to see it fall into disrepair over the past several years. As much as she had come to know Gertrude Harrison as more of a friend than an employer, she knew her faults through and through and being miserly was one of them. The old spinster had refused to spend a dime on the place in the past five years and it had pained Hannah to see the place going to ruin. She was delighted to hear that Sarah was willing to spend some money to bring Harrison House back to its former glory.

"Why of course I do. My friend's son, Patrick Gallagher, is excellent. He knows all about these old places and he is as honest as the day is long. He'll give you a fair price for his work and he will do the job right. I'll guarantee it. Do you want me to call his mother and ask her to send him over to meet with you this afternoon?"

"That would be fine."

Before any contractor arrived Sarah planned to make a list of the obvious work that needed to be done so she could compare it to the contractor's estimate of the necessary repairs. She was young, but life on her own for the past seven years had taught her not to throw away money. If the work wasn't necessary it wouldn't be done. All she wanted to do was to make this place marketable so she could sell it quickly and move back to her life in Boston.

She decided that she would start with an examination of the attic. If the roof was leaking she would be able to see signs of it there. She went to the third floor and opened a large oak door that led to the attic. She switched on a light and walked up a narrow set of creaking stairs. The air was stale and the entire space was covered in dust and cobwebs. This place is scary she thought as she made her way further into the attic. She held a flashlight in her hand and pointed the beam of light towards the ceiling. On the wooden rafters she saw some discoloration. Was that a sign there had been water coming in? She walked around the rest of the attic looking for signs of potential roof damage. But after 15 minutes in the hot dirty space that lacked fresh air, she decided she'd had enough. She went down to the third floor where there were six bedrooms each with its own ensuite bath which was unusual for Victorian homes. They'd been added by Gertrude's mother in the 1920's because she had an obsession with hygiene and privacy, Hannah explained.

As she wandered through each room she noted the beautiful hardwood furniture, heavy silk drapes and fine craftsmanship of the well constructed home. The only things needed were to remove the faded and ugly wallpaper that looked as though it had been put there in the 1970's. It was hideous in a home of this vintage. For the past seven years Sarah had taken courses on interior design and décor and knew what this place needed was to bring it back to the Victorian era.

By lunchtime she was finishing up with her inspection of all of the rooms in the home. She returned to the kitchen to find Hannah baking bread. "Sit yourself down now girl. I have made you a nice bowl of soup and a salad."

Hannah placed it on the table along with some freshly baked warm bread she'd just taken out of the oven. It smelled delicious and Sarah didn't hesitate to sit down and eat.

"Thank you Hannah. This bread is so delicious!"

Hannah smiled. She loved nothing better than compliments on her cooking. As Sarah ate she wondered how she should broach the subject of Hannah's employment. She didn't want or need a housekeeper. She decided the best approach was to be honest with the elderly woman.

"Hannah, I want to thank you so much for everything you have done to look after the house since Cousin Gertrude's passing. Please tell me what your salary is and I will be happy to pay you. You should know though that I don't plan to live here. As soon as the place is ready to show I will put it on the market and sell it so I can return to Boston."

Hannah looked surprised and saddened for a moment. She pulled a chair from the table and asked Sarah to sit down with her.

"I first came to this house when I was 20. Just off a boat from Ireland and in need of a place to stay and a steady job. I did the cooking and some of the cleaning with the help of another girl. This place was always filled with people. The Harrisons held grand parties. Sure, the work was hard but I loved it here. When the Harrisons hired me, they provided me with a good salary along with me room and board. When I fell in love with and married the Harrisons' chauffeur, they allowed him and me to take the apartment over the garage," Hannah smiled.

"My Joe and I loved working for the Harrisons but we retired 20 years ago. After 30 years of employment here, the Harrisons invited us to continue to live in the apartment and out of habit we continued to do what we have always done around here. The Harrisons provided us with good salaries. We were careful with our money and we invested it. We didn't need to be here. We wanted to be. When Gertrude's parents, Donald and Suzanne Harrison, died, she seemed to draw even closer to us. She never married and had become set in her ways. Gertrude and I came to be very good friends even though she was much older than me. As she grew older, her need for my companionship increased to the point that she seemed lost without me. My Joe died five years ago, bless his heart. So it was just me and Gertrude on this big estate and two old women can't do all that needs doing around here. That's why the place has started to go to hell with itself," she added with a sigh.

"I am pleased you're fixing the place up but I can't say that I am happy about you selling it. If you don't mind a little advice, only an idiot with their head up their arse would sell off their family's heritage and that's what you'd be doing if you sell Harrison House. I think if you got to know it better and find out who came before you here, you'd think twice about selling it all away to strangers who don't give a flying fig about your family's history. Now I have said my peace and I will say no more. If you want me out of the apartment I understand," she said with a slight quiver in her voice that told Sarah the old woman was worried about having to leave the place she considered to be her home.

The truth was it was Hannah's home. She had poured her blood, sweat and tears into this place for most of her life; so had her husband. She deserved to be here for as long as she wanted.

"Hannah I might not want to be here but I know this is your home and I have no plans to see you move out. I can make your remaining in the apartment for as long as you wish a requirement of the sale's agreement. Would you like that?"

Hannah squared her shoulders and got up from the table. "As you wish; now if you don't mind I have more bread baking in the oven that's going to burn if I don't take it out."

Sarah's offer for Hannah to remain in the apartment did nothing to address the old woman's need to continue to cook in this kitchen; her kitchen. Unsure of how to address this Sarah decided it was best not to say anymore about the subject for now. As she finished the soup she picked the bowl up from the table and took it to the sink.

"Now don't go worrying about the dishes girlie. I'll take care of that."

The doorbell rang. "I'll get that," Sarah said as she left the kitchen. It rang once more as she made her way from the kitchen at the back of the house, down the hallway and to the foyer. She looked through the peep hole in the door and saw a tall, muscular, dark-haired man. She opened the door but the chain lock kept it from opening all the way. She looked through the small opening.

"Can I help you?"

The man smiled. His teeth were perfectly straight and white. His golden brown tan showd he spent a lot of time outdoors. "I'm Patrick Gallagher," he said. "My mother's friend Hannah called and asked me to come over to have a look around and give you an estimate on some repairs."

"Okay, just a minute." Sarah closed the door and slid back the chain that barred his entrance. She opened the door and invited him inside.

"Hi. I'm Sarah Harrison," she said as she extended her hand. He shook it and stepped into the foyer.

"Hi. Patrick Gallagher," he repeated.

Sarah invited him inside and closed the door. She lead the way through the foyer into one of the home's two parlors. She invited him to take a seat and then she sat down on one of two winged back, velvet upholstered chairs.

"Mr. Gallagher, since you know Hannah you are likely aware that I have recently inherited this property and obviously it needs some work. She tells me you do renovation and restoration work. I need you to go over the entire building from attic to cellar and give me an estimate on what it's going to cost to restore the place."

Patrick Gallagher knew Harrison House well. He had come here often from the time he was a baby with his mother when they would visit with Hannah, either at the apartment above the garage or inside the kitchen. He loved everything about the place. The grounds were spectacular. That is to say they *were* spectacular when Joe Harrison took care of them. Even though he was the Harrisons' chauffer he had a passion for plants and, with Mr. Harrison's permission, was always doing things to improve the property.

Patrick looked around the parlor. It was filled with hand-crafted New Brunswick furniture made by artisans such as Thomas Nesbit. Patrick, who held a PhD in antiquities, had a passion for locally made furniture. He was especially fond of pieces by Nesbit who was the Duncan Phyfe of New Brunswick. The quality of his work equaled any made on the continent during that period.

Haunted Heart / Laverne Stewart

Nisbet followed closely the contemporary styles of his time. Splendid examples of his sideboards and card tables with spiral-twisted legs and posts and sofa tables were in this room and likely throughout the rest of the home and were highly sought after by private collectors and museum curators around the world.

Recently, one of Nesbit's card tables sold at auction for an impressive $17,000. Patrick estimated the pieces in this one room alone would sell for $60,000. This pretty young thing was sitting on a fortune in antiques, he thought to himself.

The architecture of this home was stunning. When it was built in the early 1800's, the wealthy spared no amount of money to create what might be considered by some to be palaces. Harrison House was no exception. Yes it needed a lot of work but as he looked at the bones of the house, he could see the potential to bring the home back to its original glory.

Sarah stood up "Would you like to take a look around and see what you think?"

Patrick followed her lead and stood as well. "Sure. Where do you want to start?"

"Well, I had a peek in the attic and I think there is water getting in there. Why don't we start there and work our way through the house until we get to the foundation."

"Sure thing. Let's go."

It took several hours for Sarah and Patrick to go through every inch of the place. *He's very thorough,* she thought as he examined the smallest of details and took notes as he went.

By the time they were finished, Sarah was hot, sweaty and dehydrated. She suggested they go into the kitchen for a cold drink. There they found a pitcher of lemonade in the refrigerator and a note from Hannah saying there was a plate of sugar cookies on the kitchen table under a linen napkin and that they should help themselves. Sarah found a couple of tall glasses and removed some ice from the freezer. She poured lemonade in the glasses and invited Patrick to have a seat at the table. Neither said another word as they gulped the icy-cold beverage until their glasses were empty.

"Ah. That's better! I was so thirsty," he said. Then he helped himself to a cookie. Patrick loved Hannah's cookies. When he was a boy he would help himself to them and would fill his pockets with them whenever he came for a visit. Hannah knew but said nothing more than "A mouse must be in my pantry. I think it's been eating my cookies again."

"Hannah's a fabulous cook. I think I'm going to gain weight while I'm here because she insists on feeding me and often," Sarah said as she poured more lemonade into their glasses.

"I wouldn't worry about it. You look fine to me but a bit more padding wouldn't hurt either. Don't you know that most men like girls with curves?" Patrick followed up this up with a grin and a wink which caused Sarah's face to redden slightly as she tried to ignore the remark and get on with the business at hand.

She was a beautiful woman and was used to men who flirted but she wasn't confident enough in herself to hold her own with them. This is why she rarely dated. She had gone out steadily with one of the guys from her interior design classes but it never went past the hand holding stage.

Sarah and Chaz Alvarez ended up being very good, albeit platonic, friends. About a year later he ended up coming out of the closet and since he'd admitted to himself and others his sexual orientation, they were even closer because he was no longer pretending to be someone he wasn't.

She studied Patrick's features. *Oh yes, Chaz would find you very appealing,* she mused. Wide shoulders, muscular chest, big biceps, small waist, tight butt and muscular thighs; what was not to like? This man was incredibly handsome with the bluest sapphire colored eyes that seemed to look right into her soul when he was listening to her, she thought.

Patrick continued to look at her and she looked out the window avoiding his gaze… those eyes, too intense, she thought. She broke the silence when she stuttered slightly and said "S-s-so when do you think you can give me an estimate on the work that needs to be done here? Keep in mind I am studying interior design and can help you with a lot of the work."

Patrick smiled and wanted to tease her again but he kept his comments to himself. *It would be very nice to be working closely with the red-head with a body that could make most men weak in the knees.* "I'll do that," Patrick said as he stood and picked his clip board and pencil off the table. "I'll figure out the cost of materials and labor and get back to you with an estimate by tomorrow if that's okay with you."

"Yes thanks, that would be fine. If we can come to an agreement on the cost of the work how soon could we get started?"

"You're in luck. A job that had been scheduled to start in a couple of days has fallen through because the homeowner has died and the children are squabbling now about whether to go forward with the contract. So until that gets straightened out, I'm all yours," Patrick looked at her with a smile and a wink. The innuendo made her blush again.

"Okay then, umm well, you get back to me on the estimate and I'll decide whether we can go forward with this. Nice to meet you Patrick," she said extending her hand and trying to seem unaffected by this man.

"Ms. Harrison," Patrick put his hand in hers and gave it a squeeze. "Talk to you very soon."

Sarah closed the door and watched as Patrick Gallagher walked down the pathway toward the street and a shiny black pick-up truck. If ever there was an Irish rogue he was one; tall, muscular, handsome and a real flirt. She wondered what kind of lover he would be. "Likely as hot as the very devil himself" she said, letting out a breath she'd been holding since he walked out the door.

"What have you gotten yourself into this time Sarah," she could hear her mother's chiding words in her head.

"I don't know mom but it could be fun finding out."

3

It was 4:30 and Hannah was back in the kitchen preparing supper. Sarah wondered what she should do until then. She wandered into the library. Floor-to-ceiling shelves were filled with ancient looking hard covered theological and historical text books. Then she saw something that caught her eye. It was the Harrison family history dating back to the family's arrival in Saint John from England in 1835.

Shipbuilder and Captain Cornelius Harrison, his wife Ethel, their seven-year-old son Jonah and their four-year-old daughter Evelyn Elizabeth had arrived on the newly launched *Caroline* on June 12, 1835. They had moved into the four storey home Cornelius Harrison had built and insisted be ready and fully furnished with the best that money could buy in the city.

The information in the genealogical record was slim at best. Cornelius Harrison died in his sleep in 1850. His wife passed away four years later. Evelyn Elizabeth Harrison, the record stated, had died on July 6th, 1847 at the age of 16. It made no mention of what caused the young woman's death. She decided to do some archival research. She entered the Saint John City Library's web site and articles from the New Brunswick Courier from the days following Evelyn Elizabeth's death.

As she read one article after another it seemed as though she was getting nowhere. Then a headline caught her attention. "Police Investigate the death of Ship Builder's Daughter."

Haunted Heart / Laverne Stewart

The paragraphs that followed said that investigators were looking into the death of Evelyn Elizabeth Harrison whose body had been discovered in a third floor bedroom of her father's mansion by a servant early one Sunday morning. The article then said police were trying to determine whether the girl died of natural causes, if it was accidental or murder.

Sarah hugged herself and thought of the dream she'd had the night before of the young woman who was crying. Was her dream a coincidence or was Evelyn Elizabeth trying to speak to her in her dreams as Hannah had insisted. That was nonsense. Of course it was just a coincidence. This unfortunate girl who died so young wasn't trying to reach beyond the grave for her help. Or was she?

Sarah wandered out of the library and down the long hallway toward the second parlor. She stood beside the table grand piano and looked at Evelyn Elizabeth's photo. "What happened to you?"

Hannah came into the room and heard the question. "Oh the poor thing; she died so young. Are you ready for supper? It's on the table." Sarah followed the little old woman down the hall and inhaled the aroma of what she thought might be chicken. She sat down and Hannah brought enough food to the table for a large family.

"It's hard to cook for one or two when you've spent a lifetime cooking for big crowds. There'll be plenty of leftovers for lunch tomorrow. Right then girlie, eat while it's hot."

"Hannah please sit down and eat with me."

The old woman took a plate from the cabinet and served herself some roasted chicken, mashed potatoes and vegetables too. "Hannah, when you told me you believe

Evelyn Harrison's spirit is here, were you joking or were you serious?

"Oh my dear I never joke about things like that. No. It's true. Evelyn is with us."

When Sarah was a child she used to believe that angels and the spirits of those who've passed were real but her parents discouraged her whenever she spoke of these things. In fact, her mother told her that people would think she was strange if she discussed it. They told her it was silly and that she was to put it out of her mind.

"So, if it's real then why is she here?"

"As I told you earlier, sometimes spirits don't cross over if they died suddenly and don't know they are dead or they die with unresolved issues."

Sarah told Hannah that she had done some research on her ancestors and learned that Evelyn Harrison died suddenly in her bedroom. "Did you know that?"

"Yes, so I've been told. She was found in the room you slept in last night."

"She was?" Suddenly Sarah felt a chill come across her whole body. Well, even if there are no such things as ghost she didn't want to sleep in the same room that someone had died in. And what if she'd been murdered? Creepy. Tonight she was going to sleep in another room.

Hannah took a bite of chicken, shrugged and chewed her food. "Your family has a very interesting history girlie and when you learn from the past, there are so many good things that can happen in the present and the future. Rather than me muddling things up with the bits and pieces I have heard, why don't you do a wee bit more reading and you might discover the answers to your questions."

After supper was over Sarah tried to help clean up but Hannah shooed her out of her domain once again and told her that there were so many things to discover in this place that she'd best go off and explore. So Sarah climbed the stairs to her bedroom. As she walked she felt like she did as a young girl, frightened by the unseen and yet very real and scary monsters hiding in closets and under beds.

"Oh grow up Sarah. The only thing haunting you is all of the work you know needs to be done on this old ark of a house and how much it's going to cost."

Sarah wanted to find out what had killed Sarah but she knew that would have to wait. Earlier in the day she had unpacked her clothing and placed them in dresser drawers and the large walk-in cedar closet in what used to be Evelyn Harrison's bedroom. Now she wanted to get her things out of there and move to another bedroom. She threw everything that was in the dresser back in her suit cases.

Next, she opened the closet and started taking everything out of it. As the last of the clothing was removed from the closet she was about to shut the door when she noticed that one of the boards she was standing on near the back of the closet was loose. She bent down and took a closer look. It looked like something was beneath the board. She went to the bathroom and got a metal fingernail file from her cosmetic bag. She returned to the closet and knelt down once more. She used the file to pry the oak board free. After several attempts to remove the board, it was loosened enough so she could lift it from the rest of the flooring.

There was a wooden box tucked in the space between the floor joists. Carefully she lifted it out. It was covered in dust. She blew on it and then used her sleeve to wipe the dirt away. She tried to remove the lid but it was locked. She looked back in the space where the box had been but she could see no sign of a key. What was in that box? Sarah couldn't stand a mystery. First she found out that a teenaged girl had died in this bedroom and now she's found a locked box. She was determined to get to the bottom of this.

"What happened to you Evelyn?" Just then Marmalade sprang out from the other side of the closet and landed right in front of her.

"Ahhh! You are going to give me a heart attack if you keep that up fur ball! Get out of here!!!"

Sarah stood up and brought the wooden box with her. She would either have to find the key somewhere in the room or find a way to pick the lock. Within an hour she had moved all of her belongings to the bedroom down the hall. She looked outside and then checked her watch. It was 7 p.m. She decided to make herself a cup of tea and then search the city library's online archives for more information about Evelyn's death.

The New Brunswick Courier had no reference to Evelyn Harrison's death until July 10, 1847. The headline read Overdose of Laudanum Causes Death of Shipbuilder's Daughter. The article went on to say that a doctor's prescription of the medication was taken in excess which caused the young woman's heart to fail within an hour after she'd taken the overdose of medication. What wasn't known was whether the overdose was accidental or taken on purpose.

Sarah wondered what laudanum was so she Googled the word and found an online medical dictionary which described its history and use. "Laudanum is a type of opium drug, made into an alcohol solution. It was a preferred drug of the Victorians but the highly addictive nature of opium caused many people throughout the 19th century to become quickly dependant on it. But the medication was sold and used with little regard for its possible addiction. The drug was sold in a variety of medical preparations, which were easily obtained and were inexpensive. Some popular brands of the time included Battley's Sedative Solution, Mother Bailey's Quieting Syrup, and Godfrey's Cordial. Doctors recommended it for everything from head colds, to menstrual cramps and to calm the nerves of distraught ladies and to quiet fussy babies."

So she died from a drug overdose. The historic newspaper article had speculated whether it had been an accident or murder. Maybe she could coax something more from Hannah. She had a feeling the old lady knew the full story but wasn't about to share for some reason.

She looked at her watch. It was almost 8 p.m. She realized she'd been in the house all day and she needed some fresh air. As the May sun wouldn't go down for a while longer, she decided to take a walk around the grounds. She laced up a pair of sneakers and put on a sweater. While it was blistering hot further inland, Saint John was located directly on the Bay of Fundy and it was like living in an air-conditioned city. When she stepped outside she could see the fog rolling in off the bay. It wouldn't be long before the fog would shroud the property in an eerie veil.

Sarah strolled through the gardens. They would have been gorgeous when Joseph Sullivan tended them. There were roses and perennial beds. Near the back door where the kitchen was located there was an herb garden with almost every kind of aromatic, medicinal and a wide variety of culinary herbs which any chef would be thrilled to have at their disposal. Fresh herbs. So that's why Hannah's cooking was so exceptional. Everything tasted so fresh and flavorful and this was one of the reasons why.

Next, she strolled through a walking path that was shaded in tall, mighty oak trees. She stopped and ran her hands over the bark. There were initials carved in the bark but time had made them almost impossible to detect. She traced the letters with her fingers. She thought they were EEH and PRG. Evelyn Elizabeth Harrison? But who was PRG? She had only been here 24 hours and so much had happened since then.

The fresh air and exercise from walking the grounds for the past hour had helped her to relax and feel tired. She could see a light on above the garage. That would be Hannah. *I wonder what she does up there all by herself?* Maybe she would knock on her door and thank her once again for everything she had done today. She climbed the stairs that were located on the outside of the building and knocked on the door. The door opened. Hannah was still dressed as she had been earlier in the day and was still wearing an apron.

"I hope I'm not disturbing you Hannah but I wanted to thank you once again for everything. You've been so kind and I don't know when I have eaten so well. You know I work in a very exclusive Boston restaurant and the chefs there could benefit from some cooking lessons from you. I found your herb garden when I went for a walk this evening. So that's why everything tastes so fresh and delicious."

Hannah laughed and her wrinkled face beamed with delight at the compliment. "Well the fresh herbs help dearie but the secret to great food is the love the cook adds to it. Now where did I leave my manners? Please come inside. It's getting to be cool from the fog and damp night air. I was just about to make tea. Come in, come in. It's so nice to have you in my home."

"Are you sure you don't mind? It's not too late?"

"No dear. My home is your home. Put your feet up and relax."

Sarah knew she was talking about this apartment but somehow she felt the main house really belonged to this woman and not her. What right did she have to the place? Sarah realized she barely knew the place and was about to sell it and its contents to the highest bidder. Suddenly she felt like an intruder.

"No never you mind dearie. You put those thoughts right out of your head. All will work out in the end. Of that you can be sure."

Sarah was sure she hadn't spoken aloud. Was she talking about her guilt about selling the place or was she talking about coming in on her this late?

"It's nice to have the company. Night time when it's quiet is when I miss my Joe the most. This is chamomile tea. I take a cup of it every night. It helps me to sleep. That Sleepy Time is pretty much the same thing. But this tea is made from the Chamomile I grow in the garden. It is so much better than anything you can buy. She poured the loose herb into the tea pot and added boiling water. After allowing it to steep she placed a strainer over each tea cup which helped to collect most of the tea leaves. But some went into the cups anyway. Hannah added a spoonful of honey and stirred each cup before she handed one to Sarah.

Both women sipped the hot brew in silence for a minute and then Sarah broke the silence with a question. "When I was in the garden I came across a tree with initials carved into the bark. EEH and PRG. I think the first belong to Evelyn. Do you know who PRG is?"

"That's the mystery isn't it girlie. Find out who PRG is and you will find the answers to many questions."

Sarah wasn't sure what the old lady was talking about and she was getting a little bit frustrated by her elusiveness. She was sure Hannah was holding back with the story of this place. "Please tell me the story of Harrison House Hannah. Please!"

"Darlin' sometimes the most important things we discover have to be done without the help of others. Look around. Open your ears, mind and heart to this place and you will find all of the answers you want and more."

When their tea was finished Hannah picked up Sarah's cup. "My granny taught me how to read tea leaves when I was a girl in Ireland. Would you like me to read for you tonight? Just for a few giggles and nothing more."

Sarah's mother had frowned on things such as this. She called those people who could see into the future and who had the ability to connect with the dead sinners. But Hannah was kind and thoughtful. She'd given her life to make those around her more comfortable. Sarah thought that Hannah was closer to a saint than a sinner; more than most people she knew.

"Sure. Why not. I'd love to know what the leaves have to say about my future."

Hannah looked into the cup. She was very quiet for a long time. And then she looked up and smiled. "Oh this is good. Very, very good! I see this house. It is beautiful once more. Everything is back to the way it used to be. And there is a wedding in the garden. A beautiful bride and a handsome groom are exchanging their vows and there's a baby. A beautiful red-haired baby girl. It's your wedding Sarah. It's your baby and it's going to happen very soon."

Marriage? Baby? Hannah Sullivan must have been sipping something stronger than tea. "You're joking Hannah! Ha! That's funny. The only man I have gone out with in the last year and a half is gay. He is more likely to be the one wearing a wedding gown than me. No, there is no man in my life and not the slightest chance of me having a baby. Hannah, your Granny didn't do a very good job of teaching you to read tea leaves. I'd have a better chance of being struck by lightning than getting married and becoming a mother believe me."

Hannah and Sarah both yawned. The chamomile tea was taking effect. Sarah stood up and walked to the door. Thanks for the tea Hannah and the laugh. That was fun. I'll see you in the morning. "Me, a wife and mother and soon you say? That's the funniest thing I've heard in a long time. Goodnight Hannah." Sarah hugged her and then walked down the stairs and toward the main house. The old woman stood and watched until she saw the back door open and Sarah go inside and close the door.

"Yes Evelyn Elizabeth.," Hannah said softly, "I agree. She will make a beautiful bride and I think motherhood will suit her too. I'll do my part and you do yours and we'll see that everything works out in the end. Now don't you fret girlie. I know it's been a long time coming but what you've been waiting for all these years is about to happen."

4

The sun shining through her bedroom windows woke Sarah the next morning. She'd had a peaceful sleep with no nightmares. When she got up she noticed it was 8 a.m. and thought likely she'd find Hannah in the kitchen. She put a cotton bathrobe over her nightgown and walked downstairs to the kitchen where, sure enough the old woman was preparing breakfast. "Good morning Hannah!"

Sarah's mood was bright and she was looking forward to the day. She saw that there was coffee ready. There was nothing like freshly brewed coffee ready when you woke up. "Good morning to you girlie. And how are you this fine morning? Sit down and have some coffee while I finish making your waffles. By the way Patrick just called. He has your estimate ready and he said to tell you that he'll be here later this morning with it.

"Ooh Hannah those waffles smell delicious! You are spoiling me. I usually eat canned soups and cereal. I'm not much of a cook. Maybe you could teach me how to make these."

Hannah loved the praise of her culinary skills. She served the waffles with sausage and fresh fruit. This truly was better than anything the chefs prepared at The Green Onion where she'd been a waitress for the past seven years. Over the next hour she and Hannah chatted about the city and Sarah decided that she wanted to see some of the historic landmarks while she was here. She went back up to the third floor to get showered and dressed. By 10 a.m. she heard the doorbell ring.

Sarah bounded down the stairs to answer the door, but by the time she made it to the foyer, Hannah had already opened the door to let Patrick inside.

"Sarah wants to see some of the city Patrick. I thought you might want to take her for a stroll through the City Market this morning."

"Sure. That would be fine," Patrick replied. "We can go through the market and then perhaps we can grab a bite to eat while we're there and go over the estimate."

Hannah didn't approve of the lunch plans at all. "You'll not find anything there any better than what I can make here for you. Take her to the market Patrick and when you're ready to eat I'll have a nice lunch waiting for you right here. Now go on with the pair of you. I have work to do and I can't waste anymore time standing around."

Patrick grinned and kissed the old lady on the cheek. She was his mother's best friend and like an aunt to him. "Yes Maam. We're going now."

"And don't go spoiling your appetites while you are there. Do you hear me?"

Both Patrick and Sarah laughed as they said 'Yes Hannah. See you later."

Patrick held the front door for her and she walked out into the bright sunshine. His pick-up truck was parked on the street. He got to the passenger side one step ahead of her and opened her door. "Why thank you sir!" Sarah smiled.

Patrick got in the driver's seat and started the truck. On the 10-minute drive to the market Patrick thought he should give her a bit of background on one of the most popular attractions in the city: "It was built in 1876 and managed to survive the Great Fire of 1877. Most of the city burned to the ground but somehow the city market survived. When the city was rebuilt, it did so right around the market's walls and its iron gates.

"The market is huge. It was a full city block in length. At both entrances hang the same gates that have swung closed at the end of each business day since 1880. The market is the oldest continuing farmer's market in Canada and is the historic centerpiece of the city's centre."

Sarah was impressed by Patrick's knowledge. "How do you know so much about its history?"

"It's kind of an obsession of mine. I have loved the city's history ever since I was a kid."

"Did you know," Patrick continued, "that in 1785 the King of England granted a Royal Charter allowing the operation of public markets in the city? It named the city's mayor at the time as Clerk of the Market and gave him power to grant licenses to farmers, craftsmen and others to sell their goods. Every morning and evening since it first opened a market bell is rung to signal its opening and closing. There have been many renovations and improvements like a new concrete floor, a glassed-in eating area and an indoor underground connection to Brunswick Square, a nearby mall. It's open year-round six days a week but Saturdays are the busiest day which you will soon see."

They parked the truck in an uptown parking garage just a block away from the market and walked there in a couple of minutes. As soon as they walked through the large city market doors they were standing shoulder-to-shoulder with other weekend buyers and sellers. Sarah inhaled the many delicious aromas. First she could smell fresh homemade cakes, pies and breads.

The further into the market they went they were met with other aromas; vegetables, fruit, seafood and something called dulse.

"What is that smelly stuff?" she asked as she curled up her nose in disgust.

Patrick laughed. "Hey Gerry, she's never tried dulse before. Is it okay if I give her a sample?"

"Sure. Try it. You'll love it," the balding man with the broad smile said to Sarah.

Patrick picked up a piece and handed it to her. "It's basically dried seaweed. A lot of people love it. It is really salty but it is high in iron and really good for you. Go ahead. Try it." Sarah looked suspiciously at the black, dry, smelly offering. "You're a chicken...bawk, bawk, bawk..." Patrick taunted.

Sarah hated to be teased and especially hated people to think she was afraid of anything. She shut her eyes and opened her mouth and chewed. Within a second her eyes opened very wide. She made a face in disgust and reached for tissue in her purse to spit out the offensive thing that was making her gag.

Gerry and Patrick, who'd been watching her eat it, howled with laughter. "It's an acquired taste, right Gerry."

"Yeah Patrick, you're right. It takes some getting used to," he said as he wiped away the tears that came to his eyes from laughing so hard.

Sarah needed water to rinse the foul taste from her mouth. She looked and saw a cooler filled with sodas, juice and water. She reached in and helped herself to a bottle and placed money on the counter to pay for it. She didn't speak again until half of the water in the bottle was gone. "You think you're funny do you? Well if there's one thing you should know about me Gallagher is that I have a long memory and I always get revenge."

"Is that so Harrison? Well for your information I like a woman who likes to fight back. I bet you can be a real hell cat when you get all hot and bothered." He gave her the once over and laughed again before he reached for another piece of dulse and ate it, rubbed his stomach to let her know how good he thought it was.

She rolled her eyes and walked ahead of him. Because it was so crowded they quickly became separated.

Ten minutes later he found her standing in front of a craft market where a woman was selling handmade candles and other decorative items. Sarah was picking them up and smelling the various scents. Something tickled the back of her neck. She turned round to find Patrick holding a yellow rose.

"Did you know that the yellow rose is the symbol of friendship? I am sorry Gerry and I played the mean trick on you. Like I said, dulse is an acquired taste. Some day you might like it. But until then I promise I will never goad you into eating it again. So are we friends?"

Sarah reached for the rose and as she took it from his hand her fingers touched his and she felt a shiver go down her spine. This guy was smooth. *I bet his email and Facebook accounts are filled with names and numbers of women,* she thought to herself.

As they continued to make their way through the market, Patrick introduced Sarah to many of the vendors and lots of shoppers too. He'd been coming here with his mother every Saturday morning for as long as he could remember. It was a part of the city's heritage he held dear and he delighted in sharing it with Sarah as she experienced this place for the first time.

It was almost noon when they made their way back to the truck. Patrick opened her door for her and gave her his hand so she could get up into it. "We'd better get home soon. Hannah will have a fit if we're late and lunch is spoiled. She's like an aunt to me. She and my mom have been best friends for a long time. She's always treated me like the kid she never had."

He turned the radio on. They drove in silence for a while as the Rolling Stones song *Paint It Black* played. Sarah stared out the truck's passenger window and thought about Hannah's belief that Harrison House was haunted and about her visit to Hannah's apartment when she read the tea leaves. She smiled to herself and thought just how silly all of that was. Patrick pulled the truck up beside the curb in front of the massive dwelling, then he got out and opened her door for her. "Thank you. You are such a gentleman."

Patrick smiled and winked before he said "Not always" in a rather suggestive way.

Sarah could feel herself blush again as she walked ahead of him and she tried to ignore the laughter her response brought out in this very tall, sexy-as-hell man.

She walked up to the front door and opened it with a key. "Hello Hannah we're back!"

But Sarah's greeting was met with silence. She and Patrick walked through the house and down the hall leading to the kitchen. Hannah wasn't there. Instead they found a large wicker basket on the kitchen table with a note on the top which read:

Haunted Heart / Laverne Stewart

Hello girlie and Patrick dear. I should have mentioned it to you this morning but my card club meeting is this afternoon at St. Anthony's and it's my day to prepare the luncheon. It is a beautiful day and the two of you could stand to get outside and enjoy the sunshine. It's a rare day in May when we get this kind of sunshine and heat so go out into the garden and find a shady spot under those old oaks. Spread the blanket on the ground and enjoy everything that I have prepared for you in the basket.

- Love, Hannah.

Patrick opened the basket and inside they found enough food to feed six people. Patrick's stomach growled loudly.

"Whoa. Sorry. I haven't eaten since last night. This stuff looks so good. So do you want to take Hannah's advice or should we just eat it here?"

Sarah laughed. "From the sounds coming from your stomach I'd say you'd better start eating as soon as possible but I think we'd better do as Hannah instructed and go outside to eat this. She went to the trouble to fix a picnic lunch and I think we'd likely be in trouble if we don't do as the note instructs don't you?"

Patrick reached inside the basket and grabbed a brownie and took a bite. "You're right. We should but I need a snack to give me some energy to make it to the garden. Want one for the road?"

Sarah laughed again. "No. I think I'll survive until we go outside."

Patrick picked up the basket and blanket. "After you my dear," he said before he took another bite of the brownie. They went outside and found the shady spot Hannah described in her note. It was breathtaking or it would be once the gardens were weeded and a large fountain with mermaids and dolphins was brought back to life.

Patrick placed the basket on the ground and then spread the wool Hudson's Bay blanket on the ground. "Lunch is served miss," he said pretending to be her servant. She played along and replied "Thank you Jeeves."

They ate in silence for a while. Then Patrick looked up and pointed to the roof of both the house and garage. "You were right about leaks. You're going to have to replace the shingles on both of them. The wood siding obviously needs to be scraped and painted. Some of the boards have rot and will need to be replaced. As far as the grounds go, it will need extensive landscaping. I can have a crew on all of this on Monday if you want. Like I said, an extensive restoration project just got postponed because the man that wanted the work done died last week.

As for the interior, I don't see too much structurally wrong. These houses were built to last. The electrical and plumbing had been replaced in the early 1980s. Hannah told me that was the last thing the Harrisons spent any great amount of money on here. It's a good thing they did. Replacing wiring and plumbing are huge jobs and very expensive. Gertrude Harrison obviously didn't care whether she kept the interior décor looking up to date. Walls and trim need painting and the exterior really needs help along with the landscaping.

Patrick reached into his jacket pocket and pulled out the estimate. Sarah looked at the figure on the page and swallowed. Even though she had recently inherited a lot of money and could easily afford to pay for the work, it came as a bit of a shock to see the $100,000 price tag for the restoration work that would have to be done to bring Harrison House back from the decline it had been in for many years.

"Okay. How long do you think all of this will take?"

Patrick chewed on his lower lip. He did this when he was thinking. "If I pull in some favors people owe me, I can have all of this done by late September early October. So we're talking 10 to 12 weeks. Do you want a second estimate? I can get a couple of guys who are also historic restoration experts to drop in this week."

Sarah took a long drink and was quiet for a while. She knew the sensible thing to do would be to compare Patrick's estimate to a couple of others. But Hannah said he was the best in the business and she knew that Hannah trusted him as though he was her own son. What she really wanted to do was to get this work done as quickly as possible, get the place on the market and go back to her life in Boston.

"No. I don't think that's necessary. You say you can start Monday? I want to add one thing to this before I sign it. The work must be done in the specified time. For every day you go over the deadline you'll lose a thousand dollars."

Patrick raised his eyebrows. She was young and pretty but she was no pushover. He made a note at the bottom of the contract about the penalty. "I will go back to the office and have this typed up and will be back this afternoon so we can sign it. We can ask Hannah to witness it for us."

They wrapped up the leftover food and put it back in the picnic basket. Patrick stood up and picked up the basket. He gave his hand to Sarah to help her up from the ground where she sat. She looked at her watch.

"Do you realize we have been out here for almost two hours? That was lovely. Hannah is a great cook; very delicious."

"Yeah she sure can cook but I wouldn't say the food was any better than the company. Thanks for having lunch with me Sarah. This was one of the nicest Saturdays I can remember in a long time. I'd like to do a lot more of this with you. As a rule I don't mix business with pleasure but then again, as a rule, none of my clients are as lovely as you."

Once again Sarah felt her face flush. This guy knew all the right things to say. He was extremely easy on the eyes and very good for a girl's self esteem. "Well I have never mixed business with pleasure either. But since I don't know anyone in this city besides Hannah and you it will be an awful lonely few months if I refuse your company won't it? Okay. I don't see any harm in having a bit of innocent fun with you while I am here."

Patrick gave her that look again. He didn't need to say a word. She knew "innocent" wasn't what he had in mind. With his body inches from her own she was reacting in a way that didn't feel innocent. *It could be a whole lot of fun to switch roles while she was here. Why not go from good girl to bad. What could it hurt? She wasn't going to get emotionally tied to this guy. A summer romance that ends come fall? Why not?*

Sarah could hear her mother's voice in her head: *'Sarah Jane Harrison you are not that kind of girl. What are you getting yourself into this time?'*

"I don't know mother," Sarah answered softly out loud. "But it's going to be fun finding out."

5

Patrick arrived back at the house just before six p.m. with the revised contract in hand. Sarah and he signed it in front of Hannah and she added her signature to make everything legal. She was right in the middle of preparing supper. "Patrick I am setting an extra place at the table for you. Now don't refuse or you'll break me poor old heart."

Patrick picked her up and twirled her in a circle around the kitchen floor. "I wouldn't think of it Hannah my darling."

Hannah giggled like a young girl and protested. "Put me down you young buck or I'll swat you in the arse with me dishcloth."

Patrick did as he was ordered but not before he planted another kiss on the old woman's cheek. "Now you two wash your hands and go sit at the dining table. Dinner will be ready soon."

The dining table was dressed in white linen; there was a bouquet of flowers as a centerpiece along with white taper candles. The blue and white Wedgewood china was placed at two settings along with sterling silver flatware and crystal. This was a very romantic looking scene. Both went to separate washrooms and cleaned up. When Sarah returned to the dining room Patrick pulled out a chair to seat her. As soon as he was seated, Hannah came into the room with two bowls of homemade cream of tomato soup with a hint of basil that Sarah knew must have been grown in her herb garden.

"Hannah you have outdone yourself. Why did you go to so much trouble?" Sarah asked.

Hannah smiled and looked at the two young people. "This is a very special occasion indeed. You have signed an agreement tonight that will mean Harrison House will be soon restored to its former glory. It has pained me so to see this home falling apart. Gertrude Harrison knew there were many things that needed to be done around here but in her last few years she was too miserly to part with the money to fix the place up. I am thrilled that's now going to happen. Tonight I want to toast the new life that will be breathed into this place when it gets the TLC it deserves."

She took the chilled wine and poured it into three wine glasses. She handed Sarah and Patrick the wine filled stemware and held a glass in the air. "To Harrison House!" she said lifting her glass in the air. Sarah and Patrick raised their glasses in the air too and then he had a toast of his own. "And here's to interesting new friendships," he said as he winked at Sarah.

"Okay now, you two enjoy the first course while I pay attention to what's on the stove and in the oven," Hannah said as she pushed the heavy wooden swinging door and returned to the kitchen, leaving them alone once more.

Sarah turned to Patrick.

"Patrick I found a box that had been hidden under some loose floorboards yesterday. It's locked. I haven't been able to find the key. Do you have something we could pick the lock with? I'd like to open the box to see what's inside that was important enough to hide beneath the hardwood floor in that room."

Patrick reached into his pocket and produced a set of oddly shaped long metal rods. "This ought to do the job. I keep them on me just in case I need to get inside buildings in a hurry."

Haunted Heart / Laverne Stewart

Sarah was curious. "Do you use them often?"

"Well I own several apartments and other buildings in the city and sometimes tenants lose their keys and need to get back inside in a hurry. These will also pick pad locks and safes too. After supper why don't you show me the box and we will see if we can get it open?"

So Patrick Gallagher is a landlord as well as a contractor? Interesting, Sarah thought to herself as she took another spoonful of soup. Over the next hour Hannah brought several other courses that ended with cheesecake and coffee. She came back into the dining room and started to clear the dishes. Patrick put his hand on her thin, wrinkled arm. "Hannah, you outdid yourself. You have been on your feet since early this morning. I want you to go put your feet up. Sarah and I will clear these dishes."

Hannah started to protest but Patrick knew how to get what he wanted with this woman and said "Hannah, if you don't let us clean up I promise I will never eat another meal that you cook."

"Ah, Patrick. Now don't go making threats you have no intentions of keeping. You know you can't resist me cooking."

But she agreed to leave because she thought that if they were alone to clear the dishes it would give them more time together. "Oh all right but it's only because jeopardy is on TV right now and I don't like to miss that handsome Alex Trebek. Now you two be sure to be careful with those good dishes. I'll be up in the apartment with Alex if you need me for anything; good night you two."

Hannah had cleaned up after herself as she had cooked, so there was very little to do. Sarah and Patrick put leftovers in the refrigerator. Then they filled the sink and hand washed all of the crystal and china that was too delicate to put in the dishwasher. By 8 p.m. the job was done. Patrick put a hand on his stomach and knew he had eaten too much. He needed to walk some of the rich meal off.

"It's a beautiful night. Would you like to go for a walk? It's about twenty minutes to the city's boardwalk area. There are lots of pubs that have great Celtic music. Want to walk over and have a listen? When we come back I will see whether I can open that box for you."

This had been a perfect day and Sarah wasn't in any hurry to have it end. She couldn't think of anything she'd rather do than to spend more time with him. "Sure, that sounds like fun. Give me a second to grab a sweater and I'll be ready to go."

The air was warmer than usual and the sun was still shining on their backs as they walked to the downtown bar area. They went to Grannon's and sat down at an outdoor table. Soon they were sipping on draft in large frosted mugs and listening to a band called Bottoms Up, a six-piece Celtic band that played traditional fiddle pieces as well as some Celtic inspired rock.

The music was loud which made it very difficult to have a conversation. So they watched and listened to the band through its three sets and chatted only when the band was on its three breaks of the night.

They'd been having such a great time, neither of them had paid attention to the time. When the bartender rang the bar's bell signaling last call, they looked at their watches and then at one another and laughed. After one too many beer they were both more than a little tipsy. Patrick hailed a cab and they went back to Harrison House laughing all the way home.

Sarah managed to get a key in the door and they both stumbled inside. They turned on a light in the hall and closed the front door. Sober Sarah was always shy around men she didn't know well. But drunk Sarah had very few inhibitions. "You've got a very cute butt. Do you know that? She walked up to him and put her arms around his backside and placed both hands on his rump and gave it a squeeze. "It feels as hard as it looks."

Patrick put his hands on her shoulders and moved her toward the wall and pinned her there. Then he bent down and whispered in her ear. "Don't start something you don't intend to finish."

Sarah took her hands from his butt and wrapped her arms around his neck. Her tongue licked his earlobe and she replied "I'm no quitter. Try me."

Patrick, who'd been looking at this woman's curves all day, barely concealed beneath skin-tight jeans and white T-shirt, didn't need further coaxing. He picked her up and carried her to the third floor where he located the nearest bedroom. Both felt an urgency to free themselves from their clothes, which fell to the floor. Once again he picked her up and laid her on the queen sized bed. He carefully positioned himself on top of her and bore the majority of his weight with his forearms. His tongue licked the outside of her lips urging them to open. Her eyes were closed. Clearly she was savoring the sensations he was causing her to feel as he ran his hands over her breasts. *In a couple more minutes she'll be moaning my name and begging me to go further,* he thought as his fingers lightly traced circles around her nipples. But instead of moaning he heard soft snoring.

"Sarah? Sarah?" He sat up and looked at the naked woman who'd fallen asleep just as they were about to have, what he was pretty sure would have been hot-as-hell sex, if it hadn't been for those last couple of beer she had.

Haunted Heart / Laverne Stewart

He got up from the bed and pulled on his underwear, jeans and a T-shirt. She lay on top of the bedspread so he covered her with a quilt that was folded at the end of the bed.

"You're no quitter huh? Sure you're not. Well Red, I'll take a rain check." He thought about going home for a moment but the truth was he'd had too much to drink and he knew he wasn't safe to be behind the wheel. 'Better sleep it off stud," he said to himself as he wandered down the hall to the room where Evelyn Elizabeth Harrison had died. He pulled back the covers on the bed. Soon, he too, was snoring but much louder than the snores coming from Sarah's room.

Sarah was deep in a dream... *She was looking deep into her lover's intensely blue eyes. She inhaled deeply has he bent his head down and kissed her neck. He stood behind her and as he continued to kiss her his fingers unfastened the buttons at the back of her pale pink dress. Why was she wearing this dress? And why was he dressed so strangely. A blue jacket, ruffled white cotton shirt and old-fashioned trousers?*

It didn't matter to her what they were wearing for in this moment, all she could think of was how he was making her body feel as he continued to arouse her. He whispered his desire for her as he continued in his efforts to free her from the yards of silk and ruffles of the dress that was closely fitted to the torso just under the bust and fell loosely and heavily with a full skirted below that billowed out. This dress was extravagantly trimmed and decorated with lace and ribbon. The only pleasing thing about it, in his opinion, was that it was cut low which gave him a good view of her breasts and its capped sleeves allowed him to touch the skin on her arms once he'd removed the long white gloves that reached her upper arms. He wished fashion for ladies didn't dictate that they wear layers of undergarments.

Haunted Heart / Laverne Stewart

Once the dress had fallen to the floor he concentrated on removing her chemise. It was a thin garment with tight, short white cotton sleeves and finished with a plain hem that was shorter than the dress. Next, her petticoat, which was sleeveless, and was fitted in the back with hooks and were a bugger to remove with large fingers, he discovered. When it was out of the way he concentrated on her corset which was tightly bound and made her small waist appear even smaller. When it was free so were her beautiful breasts. They were exactly as he liked them; full but not too big. They were high and firm and begging to be sucked.

He picked her up and carried her to the bed of hay. By now he could tell that she was ready. She was quivering with anticipation. He placed her gently on the bed. She watched without shame as he quickly stripped away his clothing and then joined her on the bed. They lay facing one another. It was important that he do this right for he knew this was was her first. He kissed her slowly and deeply. His tongue licked her lips and coaxed them to part. His tongue explored her mouth. She moaned and moved her hips. His hand traced lazy circles on her stomach as he moved closer to her thighs. He slipped a hand between her legs and gently pushed them apart. With his fingers he gently massaged her there. She was already wet. He sought with his mouth what his fingers had already found. His tongue darted in and out of her which she was clearly enjoying. Then he settled his mouth on her and sucked until he felt her shudder and release.

He positioned himself above her and parted her legs with his hands. Gently he entered her pushing against her maiden head. She whimpered as it gave way and allowed him to enter her fully. Together they moved as one until he could no long hold back and filled her fully with his seed and they lay together in one another's arms, both satisfied with their union...

Sarah woke the next morning thinking of the night before. She stretched and yawned and then rolled over to discover that she was alone in the bed. Where was he? She got out of bed and found her bathrobe. She went into the bathroom, showered and dressed quickly. She practically ran down the two flights of stairs and made her way into the kitchen where she found Patrick sitting at the kitchen table drinking a cup of coffee while Hannah was flipping pancakes, frying sausage and making scrambled eggs.

Patrick was quiet. Hannah made up for it. "Well good morning to you girlie. You sure slept late. Patrick and I have been keeping one another company this past hour. We thought you'd never join us. Well, you needed the sleep after the time you had last night I would imagine."

Sarah felt her face redden. How did she know they had slept together? She poured herself a cup of coffee and sat down at the table and stared at Patrick. He didn't look well.

"Yes, you young people had quite a time of it I would say."

Sarah wanted to crawl under the table from embarrassment. Even if Hannah did know they'd had sex, why didn't she keep her opinions to herself?

"Lord help him. Patrick always did suffer the morning after a good time. Come you two, start into this big breakfast and you will feel like a million dollars. Now, I've got to go. I missed mass this morning but the church is open for confession. Would either of you like to come along and clear your consciences?"

Hannah laughed and picked up her purse. "Be good. See you later." Sarah looked at Hannah and back again at Patrick who was holding his head and quietly sipping coffee.

Haunted Heart / Laverne Stewart

"Did you tell her we slept together last night? Did she enjoy all of the dirty little details?"

Patrick lifted his head and looked at her in a state of confusion. "What are you talking about?"

Sarah's mood was turning about as gray as the pallor of Patrick's skin. "How else did she know we slept together last night? I doubt she heard the moaning and sweet words you whispered in my ear all the way from her apartment. Why would you tell her we had sex?"

"I didn't tell her we had sex. I don't kiss and tell. The only love making that was done last night must have happened in your dreams. After you came on to me last night and I took you up on your offer, you passed out cold before anything happened. I slept in the bedroom down the hall from you."

Sarah insisted. She stood up and put her hands on her hips. "You removed my clothes. You laid me on the bed. You... we... well, I can't believe you don't remember what we did or was it because you drank too much to remember?"

Patrick took another gulp of coffee and stood up. His head was pounding. It was true that he'd had too much to drink and as a result he was hung over this morning. But it was also true that if he'd had the opportunity with her he certainly would have remembered making love to this gorgeous creature.

He put his hand behind her head and slipped his fingers into her mane of copper curls. He pulled her very close to him, lowered his head and kissed her very hard on her pouting red lips. "Listen Red... let's be clear on something. You invited me into your bed last night. I was happy to oblige. But I didn't get any further in the love-making department with you than kissing your pretty mouth and touching those, round, firm tits. You passed out on me. As sexy as you are, and you are very sexy Red, I do have principals and having sex with a woman who is practically comatose isn't something I stoop to. You started snoring and the moment, for me, was lost. I would have gone home but I was too drunk to drive so I went down the hall and slept in another bed. Now if you'll excuse me, I have a lot of phone calls to make today if I'm going to have a full crew here tomorrow morning ready to start this project. We'll be working mostly on the exterior first, but, if you want, you can start to move things out of the way upstairs so things can be ready when we need to get started on the interior work. I'll see you tomorrow."

6

Patrick knew he was being a jerk but at that moment he was in pain and a little annoyed with her. It had been fun to flirt a bit with Sarah but he'd signed a $100,000 contract with a deadline that would cost him money if it didn't come in on time. He needed to concentrate on what was important.

"Get your head in the game Gallagher," he said to himself as he left her standing there. All the way home he thought of how beautiful her body had looked in the pale moonlight that shone through the bedroom windows. No they hadn't made love but he sure as hell had wanted to. His unfulfilled desire for her plus the pounding headache from too much beer had made him more than a little on edge. He needed to go home, get some Tylenol and work off his frustration in the gym once he could stand without feeling like the world was spinning around him. He wanted Sarah desperately but he wanted her fully awake and begging him to make love to him. It was going to be hellish hard to concentrate on this job with her so close for these next 12 weeks.

Sarah wasn't sure what to do. She looked at the two plates of pancakes, sausages and eggs that had gone untouched. She didn't feel like eating so she scraped everything into the garbage, put the dishes in the dishwasher and went back upstairs to her room. She lay on her bed and stared at the ceiling. *They hadn't had sex? But she was sure they had. It couldn't have been a dream. She felt his hands and mouth on her. She knew she had climaxed.* She rolled over on her side and looked at the wooden box on the dresser. Patrick had promised to open it for her when they'd returned from the bar. They had other things on their minds last night and had forgotten entirely about it. But now Sarah was alone.

Haunted Heart / Laverne Stewart

She needed something to distract her from what had just happened with Patrick in the kitchen. She decided not to wait for him to open it. She got her metal nail file and stuck it into the keyhole. It didn't budge. Where was that key? She returned to what had been Evelyn Elizabeth's room.

"Evelyn if I were you where would I hide a key?" Sarah opened the closet and ran her hands over the walls and then over the wooden floor. She was about ready to give up when Marmalade ran into the room and jumped from the floor to the dresser and then to the top of an armoire. That damned cat was going to give her a heart attack. "Marmalade! You stupid fur ball! I ought to..."

Sarah stopped yelling at the cat when she noticed it was pawing at the armoire's door. Sarah walked over and opened it. She looked inside. Nothing seemed out of the ordinary. She was about to close the door when she saw something that caught her attention. At the back of the armoire were three skeleton keys. She removed the keys from a hook. She walked over to the dresser and picked up the wooden box. One-by-one she put a key in the lock to see if it would open the box. "This is silly. None of these keys is the right..." Just then Sarah felt the lock slide. She lifted the lid. Inside she found things she knew had been very dear to the girl who once lived here. First there were tiny pieces of parchment paper. On them were written poems. Whoever wrote them had obviously loved her deeply. On the first piece of paper she read:

"I am here and yet am unseen

I am not as once I've been

Now I strive to prove my worth

To live again in joy, in mirth

See the man I truly am

I will rise in wealth again."

Haunted Heart / Laverne Stewart

Who was this invisible man who needed Evelyn Elizabeth to see him for whom he really was? She read the next poem. It was so endearing. He was clearly smitten by her ancestor's beauty.

"Maiden, maiden fair of face

Eyes of green in state of grace

Voice as soft as feather down

Beauty in the pale pink gown

See me here, watch me now

You have me on my knees and how."

Why didn't any men she knew write love poems? Well Chaz would write love poems but they would be for the lucky guy he was dating these days. There were few, if any, heterosexual men alive these days that she knew who cared enough about any woman who would take the time to write words of tribute to her beauty and evidence of his complete adoration and devotion such as these.

"Boy Evelyn Elizabeth, this guy sure was hot for you girlfriend! I wish some guy would romance me this way." As she read the next poem it brought tears to her eyes.

"Lady fair from afar

I am here and there you are

My fondest wish; to kiss your face

To hold you in a warm embrace

Some day soon Lord I pray

We shall see our wedding day"

Haunted Heart / Laverne Stewart

The last poem gave Sarah some hope. It was a tribute to their love and to the future.

"Lady fair now not so far

Thanks to God here we are

My heart's desire is coming true.

My only wish: to be with you

Our lives entwined will start tonight

Meet me under pale moonlight."

Did they marry? What happened to him and why did Evelyn Elizabeth end up dead from a laudanum overdose?

Also in the box were a gold locket and a tiny watercolor portrait that someone had painted of her. Had the heart-shaped locket been a gift to her from him? Had he painted her portrait? Was he the PRG whose initials were carved in the oak tree in the garden? All of these unanswered questions were driving her crazy. She couldn't stand a mystery. Tomorrow was going to be a very busy day as the restoration work got started so Sarah decided to spend some time today concentrating her efforts on finding out more about Evelyn Elizabeth and the mysterious PRG.

She took a flashlight and walked up to the fourth floor. She opened the heavy attic door. She walked up the creaky staircase and stood at the top of the stairs. She wasn't sure what she was looking for but she was determined she wasn't going to leave this musty old space until she found something that told her more about these young lovers. She shone the light around the large space. There were old steamer trunks and a couple of cedar chests here as well as the castoffs of five generations of Harrisons. This place was

Haunted Heart / Laverne Stewart

like a dusty, cobweb covered time capsule from a few years ago and dating all the way back to the early 1800s when Cornelius Harrison and his family had moved into their new home in this new land.

She wasn't going to be able to stand another minute here unless she was able to breathe in some fresh air. There were semi-circular windows with latches at either end of the attic for cross ventilation. With a little effort she managed to get them open. The cool breeze stirred up some dust but it also cooled the attic temperature down and made her feel less claustrophobic. Once again she looked around the space and wondered where she should start first. She ruled out every cardboard box because they clearly weren't from the right era. She decided she'd have better luck with some of the steamer trunks. She tried to open the first. It was locked. She went on to the second. It was locked too. Next she tried to open one of the cedar chests. 'There is no point trying to open this one either because it will be locked too,' she said as the lid opened with ease.

As she opened the lid she inhaled the scent of cedar and she saw lots of women's clothing and it was old, very old. Could this be part of the wardrobe that Evelyn Elizabeth wore before she died? At the top of the pile she found a box. Inside there was a pale pink bonnet and white long gloves. Next she saw the same shade of pink. The fabric looked like silk. Sarah carefully lifted it out of the trunk. Was this the pale pink dress Evelyn Elizabeth's admirer wrote about? She had no idea. But what she was sure of was how tiny it was. Sarah was tall, slender. This girl, as most women were in the mid 1800s, would have been much shorter from the looks of the dress that would have been made to flow down to the floor. She folded it carefully as she set it down on the top of the nearest trunk, which she'd wiped clean with her sleeve to keep the pale pink dress from becoming soiled with dust.

Next, she found a dress that time had not been kind to. The fabric had yellowed over the passing years. Sarah didn't get excited. Not until she saw another gown. It had an emerald green satin sash. This was Evelyn Elizabeth's dress. The one she'd seen in the dream she'd had of the girl the first night she'd arrived at Harrison House.

She envisioned the beautiful young girl in this dress dancing at her first ball. She saw her in the arms of a handsome man who'd written her love poems. "What happened to you and what happened to the one you loved Evelyn?" Sarah wondered aloud. She was still thinking of the young ill-fated couple when she heard her name. It was almost a whisper.

"Sar-ah!"

"Hannah, I'm in the attic," Sarah answered. Then she heard her name again. It was very faint but she was sure someone was calling to her. *"Sar-ah! Sar-ah!"* There it was again and she also suddenly smelled the scent of wild flowers. The once very hot attic now felt cold. She had a sense that she wasn't alone. She dismissed the crazy thoughts of haunted houses and ghosts from her mind once more and decided that obviously Hannah was calling to her from a few floors below. She walked out of the attic quickly and went down into the kitchen. Hannah wasn't there. She wasn't anywhere else in the house either.

Sarah knew she'd heard a voice. This old place was giving her the willies this morning. She remembered feeling the same way when she came here as a kid but her parents had scolded her whenever she spoke of seeing and hearing things they could not hear and see so, from then until now, she'd learned to block out those feelings. Sarah decided to do a little research on the paranormal.

Haunted Heart / Laverne Stewart

She opened her laptop computer and Googled the words haunted and spirit. She found a web site dedicated to the paranormal and those who were interested in ghost-busting. She read: *"Strange, unaccountable noises, objects that inexplicably disappear only to reappear somewhere else entirely. You glimpse snatches of something and you hear footsteps in the hall when you are all alone. Odd scents permeate the air. Sometimes you feel an inexplicable chill. Guess what? It looks like you might be haunted! But don't worry. You are not alone. These encounters with the other side occur with much more frequency than anyone realizes and can affect new homes and those that are centuries old. While many people don't relish sharing their home with a ghost, some people have learned to live with their specters and rather enjoy their companionship."*

Sarah closed her laptop. "Okay that's just too weird. I'm not going to waste any more time on this nonsense. It's a gorgeous day. Why am I here reading about ghosts and worrying about something that isn't even true?" She decided she needed to go for a walk and clear her head that, in truth, was still fuzzy from the alcohol. She walked through the old city streets and marveled at the architecture. Soon she found herself at a national historic site in the city's north end called Fort LaTour which she discovered was a popular tourist attraction. A dozen other people were there with her looking at the site. Information she read on a tourist brochure described its history:

"In 1631, the governor of Acadia was named Charles de LaTour. He established a fort at Portland Port, which was near the mouth of the St. John River. The Fort was an excellent location, ideal for fur trading in New France. Madame Francois Marie de LaTour was Charles de LaTour's wife. While he was away in Boston, D'Aulnay de Charnisay attacked the fort, and on the fifth day of battle, it was finally overtaken. Madame LaTour surrendered only

under the condition that Charnisay let the men praying at the Easter Service live. He agreed, but moments later he went back on his word and killed every man in front of Madame LaTour. Madame LaTour died shortly after, and was buried near the fort, although her grave site has never officially been found. Charnisay would then go on to build Fort Saint Jean on the western side of the harbor. He died not too long after, drowning during a canoe trip on the river. Often many have said they have seen the ghost of Madame LaTour, dressed in a gray gown, walking around the former Navy Island in Jervis Bay. Several coffins have been dug up in the area, but none of these remains proved to be that of Madame LaTour. Today, the site of the fort stands as a national monument."

"Oh good grief!" Sarah had just about all she could stand of spirits and haunted places for one day.

She walked back to Harrison House more frustrated than when she'd left. *"The sooner this house is ready to sell the better,"* she thought.

When she arrived at Harrison House there was still no sign of Hannah.

Sarah walked upstairs to her bedroom. She wasn't used to drinking and late nights and after the long walk and fresh air she felt as though she needed a nap.

It wasn't long before she was asleep and dreaming again. *She was dressed in the pale pink gown she'd found in the cedar chest. She was smiling at someone. A hand reached out and kissed her palm.* "I love you Evelyn Elizabeth Harrison," the man said.

"And I love you Padraig Ryan Gallagher."

7

Sarah awoke. The name was still in her thoughts. *So Evelyn Elizabeth was in love with a man named Padraig Gallagher. It could be? No it had to be coincidental.* She needed to know more about this man. She decided to search for anyone with that name at that time. Sarah thought that likely this man and Evelyn Elizabeth were likely close in age but she had no idea whether he'd been born here or immigrated to this country. Perhaps he'd be listed in census or immigration documents. She opened her laptop and Googled his name. Lots of present day Patrick Ryan Gallagher's were listed but none from 167 years ago. Next she went into the city's library website and searched for information that would tell her how to access ships passenger lists and census records. They were available but not online. Sarah knew she would have to go to the public archives and track down Padraig Gallagher's family tree.

She arrived at the library at 4 p.m. it would be closing in an hour. It was very unlikely she would find what she was looking for in that amount of time. Still she decided to try. With the help of a very kind lady in the archival department she was able to access census records from 1830, 1840 and 1850. She looked at the papers but discovered the handwritten records were very difficult to read. With only five minutes before the library was to close she decided she'd better go home. When she arrived at Harrison House, Hannah was in the kitchen peeling potatoes.

"Well there you are girlie. I was beginning to wonder where you'd gotten yourself off to. You look a whole lot better than you did this morning. I can't understand why people drink that horrid stuff. Sure it makes you feel fine when it's going down but there's the devil himself to pay the next morning. Isn't that right Sarah?"

Haunted Heart / Laverne Stewart

So this morning she had been talking about the night of drinking and not about her and Patrick's romp in the sheets, or what she'd thought had been a night of hot and heavy passion, Sarah realized.

Hannah put the potatoes on the stove to boil and sat down beside Sarah at the kitchen table. She felt the emotional turmoil Sarah was feeling. There were a lot of things on her shoulders right now. She'd inherited a monstrously large property that needed a massive amount of work done to it, which was going to cost a small fortune to do. Then there was the matter of Evelyn Elizabeth. She knew Sarah was struggling with trying to make sense out of things not of this world.

"Sarah a couple of days ago you told me you had dreamed of the girl in the painting. Have you had any more dreams of her or has anything else unusual happened since then?"

Sarah felt a great need to talk about everything and yet she worried that she would be told she was crazy if she shared the things she'd dreamed and heard these past two days. But Hannah told her she'd heard and felt and seen Evelyn too so Sarah felt it would be safe to tell her what had been going on. "Last night I dreamed of her and a man. They were making love. Then this morning I opened a wooden box I'd found hidden in what had been her room. Inside were the love poems he'd written to her. I decided to look further to see if I could find out more about her and the man she loved so I went to the attic. I found a cedar chest with dresses that I am sure belonged to her. As I was looking at them I heard my name. I thought it was you but when I came downstairs you weren't here. I went for a walk earlier today and when I came home I decided to have a nap. Again I dreamed of the young lovers. He said to her 'I love you Evelyn Elizabeth Harrison.' And she replied 'And I love you Padraig Ryan Gallagher.' I don't understand why I'm hearing my name and why I'm having such vivid dreams about them. I feel like I'm losing it"

Hannah put her small wrinkled hand on top of Sarah's and gave it a pat. "There, there, now girl. Don't you worry about a thing. You are *not* losing it. Why, if anything, you are finding it."

Sarah didn't understand. "Finding what?"

"When you were a girl you used to tell me that you would see and hear and speak to people that others could not. Your mother told you not to talk about such things didn't she? Well what you think were imaginary friends were really the spirits of loved ones that have passed and who are always watching over you. I believe you have always been connected to Evelyn Elizabeth Harrison. Do you remember seeing a beautiful lady who would spend time with you when you were very small?"

Sarah didn't remember.

"Well girlie," Hannah continued., "I know very well that you and she were very good friends at one time. You used to tell me that she came to you to visit you in your bedroom in Boston all the time. You called her Evie. Do you remember now?"

Sarah still didn't recall it.

"Well you and she were good friends. You have blocked those memories. Most people do once they reach a certain age and others tell them it isn't normal to talk to the dead. There's nothing to fear Sarah. Evelyn is trying to talk to you. She wants you to know things and the easiest way for her to get through to you right now is in your dreams. When you heard your name this afternoon in the attic it was her, for sure."

Sarah was confused. *Why was her dead ancestor trying to talk to her now and was there a connection between Padraig Ryan Gallagher and the Patrick Gallagher she had almost slept with last night?* "Hannah have you ever heard the name Padraig Ryan Gallagher? Was he Patrick Gallagher's ancestor? What happened to them and why did she end up dead?"

Hannah shrugged her shoulders. If she knew anything she wasn't saying and changed the subject.

"Speaking of Patrick I called him after I got home from confession today. I told him I prayed for him and you after your lost night of drinking," Hannah laughed to herself.

"I told him I wasn't at all pleased with the two of you for not eating the breakfast I made for you."

Sarah was about to fib and tell her it was delicious but Hannah stopped her. "And don't tell me you ate it because the evidence of it was right there in the garbage can that I found when I was throwin' out the potato peels. Now to make it up to me I told him he will march himself right over here for supper and you will join him. Supper will be ready in an hour. Now why don't you go have a nice bath and put on something pretty. A man likes it when a woman fusses over her appearance for him."

"Hannah, Patrick Gallagher is a contractor that I have hired to restore this place. He is nothing more to me I assure you."

"Oh is that so girlie? Then why is it that when I mentioned his name you licked your lips like a cat after drinking warm cream? You can't fool me. Now go get that bath and be back down stairs in one hour. Do you hear me Sarah Jane Harrison?"

Sarah blushed and got up from the table. There was no use in arguing with Hannah. She had already figured out that despite her size and age, this woman wasn't to be tested and she always got her way.

"Yes maam."

Sarah ran the bathtub with warm water and vanilla bean scented bubble bath. She stripped her clothes and eased her body down into the water. She closed her eyes and imagined Evelyn and Padraig together. He was tall and muscular with sapphire eyes. She imagined them kissing. They lay in a field of wild flowers. Slowly they helped each other undress as they continued to explore one another's bodies. She felt his hardness on her thigh. He wanted her, of that there was no doubt. She wanted him too. But no longer was Sarah thinking about Evelyn and Padraig.

Sarah's mind was on Patrick and what she wanted him to do to her. Sarah's hand slipped beneath the water and went between her legs. She touched herself. The tiny pink nub was throbbing. She felt waves of pleasure build and build within her stomach until, with a soft moan of pleasure, she felt a huge release as the orgasm washed over and around her and through her. God she wanted Patrick. How in the hell was she going to have him near her and keep things cool and professional. It was going to be a hell of a summer.

When Sarah had finished dressing in jeans and a pink spaghetti strapped camisole and a white blouse she did her hair and put on some makeup. She didn't wear it often but a little bit of mascara helped to lengthen and darken her blond, almost invisible eyelashes. She looked at herself in the mirror. Not bad; could be better; but not bad. She came down stairs just as the doorbell rang. She looked through the peep hole in the door. It was Patrick.

Haunted Heart / Laverne Stewart

She opened the door and looked at him. He started back at her and with those deep blue eyes. He had the ability to make her stomach feel like a dozen butterflies were flying around in it. "Come in," she managed to say. After their parting this morning she wasn't sure how to behave. So she tried to act as casual as possible. She was about to turn and walk toward the kitchen when he put his hand on her shoulder.

"Sarah I am sorry about this morning. I acted like a real ass. I left here as fast as I could because I wasn't sure what else to do in that moment."

Sarah wasn't sure what to say and simply nodded her head. She too had over-reacted this morning. It was simply a case of nerves the morning after the night before that had never really happened as it turns out, much to her regret. Finally she found her voice and apologized too. Patrick put his arms around her waist and pulled her close. He placed a gentle kiss on her mouth and then looked into her eyes. Hypnotic blue eyes that could make a girl do almost anything, she thought. In this moment she felt bold. She wanted him to know that it hadn't been the beer talking last night when she showed her desire for him. Her hand reached up to the back of his head. Her fingers curled through his thick, dark hair and she pulled him down to her and kissed him again. This time she slid her tongue inside his mouth. They stood there enjoying the moment not wanting it to end but it did when they heard Hannah clear her throat to let them know that they were no longer alone.

"Well if you two can come up for air, supper is ready."

Hannah walked back to the kitchen with a smile on her face. "See Evelyn, I told you not to worry. Everything is working out exactly as it should."

Haunted Heart / Laverne Stewart

Both Patrick and Sarah blushed and then looked at one another and laughed. They felt like two kids that had been caught doing something they should not have been doing. "I'm hungry," he said as he took her hand and walked down the hall. In truth she was too. She hadn't eaten all day and whatever was for supper was making her drool. So was the sight of Patrick in those jeans and white T-shirt that brought out the color of his sun-bronzed skin.

Once again Hannah had set the dining room table with all of its finery. She served them cream of cauliflower soup, followed by a garden salad. Next she served the entree of whipped garlic potatoes, chicken divan, and orange glazed baby carrots. With coffee she served fresh strawberry pie. She refused to join them for dinner claiming that she'd already eaten. They suspected she wasn't telling the truth but both knew better than to argue with her.

"I'm leaving you two with the dishes again tonight even though I don't know whether I should trust you alone after that display in the foyer. A few of the girls from St. Anthony's are coming around tonight for a game of bridge. Don't do anything I wouldn't do now you hear?" Hannah laughed out loud at what she considered to be her very funny comment as she opened the back door and made her way to the apartment above the garage.

Patrick and Sarah lingered in the dining room over a second cup of coffee. As they cleared the table and washed the fine china, silver and crystal stemware, Sarah pretended they were married and this was something they'd been doing for many years. There was a lot she didn't know about him. Had he ever been married? How old was he?

"Ever play 20 questions?" Sarah asked.

"Yeah, do you want to play? Go first."

"Okay how old are you?"

Patrick said he'd just turned 35. "Now it's my turn. When did you have your first kiss and who was the boy?"

"That's two questions but I will allow it. I was 13 and his name Willie Zuckerman. He had braces and a lot of zits. I really couldn't stand him. It was at a party and we were all playing spin the bottle. He spun and it pointed at me. Yuck!"

"Good. I'm glad. I'd hate to think you were wishing it was Willie Zuckerman rather than me tonight."

Patrick dropped the dish towel and picked her up. He sat her on the kitchen counter so the two of them were face to face. She wrapped her legs around his waist. They kissed until she felt dizzy. He picked her up and walked with her in his arms not stopping until he had climbed both flights of stairs to the third floor and they were back in Sarah's bedroom. He put her down and looked into her eyes.

"I'd like to finish what we started last night if it's okay with you," he said. Sarah didn't answer. Instead she undid the button on his jeans.

8

"Damn girl!" Was all Patrick could think to say in the moment. They removed each other's clothing and they fell together on the bed. They were both ravenous for the other. This was raw sexual exploration. His mouth left hers and found first one pink hard nipple, which he sucked while his fingers concentrated on the other. She was breathing heavily and moaned aloud. She closed her eyes and savored the sensation. Next his tongue licked her belly as he made his way toward her inner thighs. Gently his hand coaxed her legs apart and she welcomed his exploration there. His tongue flicked back and forth and he continued to lick and suck on her there until she arched her back and cried out as she felt an explosion inside of her.

He then centered himself above her. His now throbbing hardness was demanding attention. "Do you have something? She whispered. He left her long enough to reach into the pocket of his jeans and put a condom on. He entered her. They clung to one another as they rocked back and forth like two acrobats locked in a high-wire trapeze act. He called her name. 'Sarah,' 'Sarah' and with a shudder he let himself go just as she felt a second explosion deep within her body.

They were very quiet for a while as they lay in one another's arms. He looked down at her and smiled. Then he placed a kiss on the tip of her nose. "Do you know how beautiful you are?" Sarah felt her face redden. He added: "I have made a discovery."

"What's that?" Sarah asked as she rolled over on her side.

"It's true what they say about redheads. Hot, hot, hot; like fire. Did you know that Red?"

"Yes I've heard that before and don't call me Red! Don't you know those who play with fire end up getting burned? I'd be careful if I were you." Sarah picked up a pillow and threw it at him. It missed.

"I like to live dangerously and I always play to win," he said as he kissed her mouth. From the feel of his groin on her stomach she could tell that he was far from satisfied. For the next hour they explored one another again until both had climaxed once more and they fell asleep in one another's arms.

Sarah was dreaming again... *She was in a stable. The long building housed four horses and a carriage. She wandered from one stall to another looking at the beautiful animals and petting their muzzles. She turned around as she heard footsteps approach. It was Padraig. He was carrying a riding saddle. He placed it on one of the stall doors which he then opened and led a black gelding out. He placed the saddle on the horse's back. When the horse was ready he turned to her and said 'Enjoy your ride Miss. He passed the reigns to her and their fingers touched for a brief moment.*

"Thank you Padraig. I shall."

Sarah awoke. She looked around the now-darkened room. Beside her, Patrick was sleeping soundly. *What the hell was that? Was she fantasizing of her and Patrick or was she dreaming of the love affair between Evelyn and Padraig? Had Evelyn been in love with the stable groom?*

Sarah got up and went to the bathroom. She got into the shower. The warm water felt good on her skin. She washed her body with shower gel and the suds smell of apricots made her skin feel soft and smooth. She shut off the water and stepped out of the shower. The steam from the shower had fogged up the mirror. Sarah wiped it away with her towel. She looked in the mirror. She saw her reflection and for a brief moment, she thought she saw Evelyn Elizabeth too. Sarah screamed. Loud enough to wake Patrick out of a sound sleep. He jumped out of bed and ran to the bathroom where he found her standing there, shaking and very pale.

"What's wrong Sarah? What happened?"

Sarah was still shaking when he wrapped her in the bathrobe that was hung on a hook by the shower door. She continued to shake as he led her back to bed and tucked her under the covers. "Sarah please, tell me what's upset you."

Sarah clung to him. She wasn't sure she had actually seen something or whether it was simply her imagination working overtime in the middle of the night.

"It was nothing. I'm sorry I woke you."

Patrick wasn't about to let this go.

"I'm a very deep sleeper. You screamed loudly enough to wake me up and that's pretty loud. It was something. What was it?"

Sarah decided to share everything that she had experienced since she arrived at Harrison House. "So there you have it. I think I am going crazy. I'm hearing my name being called when there's no one in the house but me. I have smelled wildflowers while in the attic which suddenly went from very hot to very cold and I've been having the most vivid dreams of my ancestor Evelyn Elizabeth Harrison. The reason I screamed is that I was sure I saw someone standing behind me as I looked in the mirror after I got out of the shower. I think I'm losing it. But Hannah says she thinks I'm finding it. She told me she believes my ancestor is trying to contact me from the other side. She says the dead often communicate with the living in dreams because it is one way we can accept their messages without freaking out. Do you believe in all that stuff? Do you think Hannah is right or is she simply an eccentric old woman who is helping to feed my over-active imagination?"

Patrick put his arm around Sarah and held her close to him. "Sarah I've known her all of my life. I think of her as family. I don't know about others who claim to have psychic abilities, but I do know Hannah. She is someone who we Irish call sensitive. She feels things. She sees things both in the past and things that are yet to happen. She has a gift that's for sure. If she tells you something is true then it's true, of that I have no doubt."

They returned to the bedroom. Sarah went to the dresser where the wooden box was. She picked it up and brought it back to the bed. "Remember I told you that I found this under some floorboards in the bedroom where you slept last night, that once had been Evelyn Elizabeth's room?" She opened the box and showed Patrick the locket, the small watercolor portrait and the love poems. He read them aloud. "Hey these are beautiful. Who wrote them?"

Sarah told him she wasn't sure but she believed that Evelyn Elizabeth was having a love affair with a servant on her family's estate and that she was sure he must have written them to her. "Why do you think that?" Patrick asked.

"Well I dreamed of the two of them and in one of the dreams she said his name. Padraig Ryan Gallagher."

Patrick stared at her. "Sarah, are you sure?"

Sarah nodded. "Yes. I have heard the name while dreaming several times. Why?"

Haunted Heart / Laverne Stewart

Patrick sat up and looked at her. "Sarah, Padraig Ryan Gallagher was the name of my great, great, great uncle."

They looked at the poems again and then at one another.

"Do you think my ancestor had a romance with your ancestor?" Sarah asked. *It was possible. They'd both lived in Saint John at the same time. Patrick knew his family tree very well but he'd never heard or read anything that would have linked his great, great, great uncle to Evelyn Elizabeth Harrison.*

"Tell me about him," Sarah said as she snuggled closer to him.

Patrick kissed Sarah on the forehead and leaned back against the pillows getting comfortable before he recounted his family history to her. "The Gallaghers sailed to Saint John from Dublin in 1846. It was the year after the great famine had begun. When the country's potato crop was rotting from the blight there was a seven-year period of mass starvation, disease and emigration between 1845 and 1852, during which the island's population dropped by about twenty-five percent. It's estimated that about one-million people died and another million emigrated from Ireland to the U.S., Canada and other countries. The potato blight struck all of Europe but Ireland was hit especially bad because a third of the population was entirely dependent on the potato for food."

"Padraig's father, Cormack Gallagher, had been a wealthy merchant and had extensive holdings in Ireland," Patrick continued. "Fearing for their safety, due to rising unrest among the poor and starving in the nation, and, like many of Ireland's privileged, he became an absentee landlord and moved his family to Saint John to find a safe haven from the lack of food and the fear of violence. He convinced his younger brother Connor Gallagher to come with them.

They emigrated from Ireland to Canada. While at sea Padraig's father, mother and one of his two younger brothers became sick with ship's fever which was an old name for epidemic typhus, which was common in the crowded conditions aboard the ships that brought the Irish and other immigrants to North America from Europe. Padraig was 18 and heir to his father's fortune. But because he couldn't claim it until he turned 21, it was supposed to have been held in trust for him by his uncle. It turns out his uncle was an alcoholic and a gambler and within a year all of land holdings had been sold and the fortune was gone. Uncle Connor, so ashamed of what he'd done, shot himself in the head with a pistol. Padraig was penniless and, for the first time in his life, knew he would have to rely on his strength and intelligence to survive in this new country and to take care of his younger brother Griffin. One of his family's businesses was horse breeding. Padraig had a passion for thoroughbred horses. His dream was to earn enough money to buy land and horses and start a new horse farm in this new land. But until then he needed to support himself. Because he was so skilled with horses he immediately found work as a horse trainer."

Sarah thought about her dream where Evelyn Elizabeth had been in a stable. She had thanked Padraig for helping to ready her horse for a ride. Was it the same Padraig? She believed it was. If it was true that he worked for the Harrison family in their stables, then he was likely there for less than a year when she died of the overdose. So what had happened to him?

"How long did he work as a groom and horse trainer?"

"Not sure. But according to the family genealogy records, he was killed in an accident with a team of horses."

There were so many unanswered questions. How had Evelyn Elizabeth and Padraig met? How long had their romance continued and what had happened to end it with their deaths? Somehow Sarah had to find the answers but it would have to wait. She looked at the clock on the bedside table. It was now 1 a.m. and they both had a busy day tomorrow. The work crew was due to start at 8 a.m.

"We'd better got some sleep. It's going to be a long day tomorrow and it will start in another seven hours," she said as she reached for the lamp switch."

Patrick had other ideas. "I think staying awake for a while longer won't hurt," he said and he kissed her mouth. Long into the night they made love.

From her apartment above the garage Hannah sat with her feet up while drinking a cup of tea. She smiled and nodded. "Yes, didn't I tell you things would be fine? We're a great team you and I. Why it won't be any time Evelyn and we'll be sending out the wedding invitations."

A loud noise woke Sarah from her sleep. She opened one eye. There was a large orange fur ball on her chest. The noise was the sound of Marmalade humming a happy tune. "Go away flea bag. I am not ready to get up yet and you aren't helping."

Sarah pushed the large cat from her. An obviously offended feline turned her back to the sleepy woman and jumped from the bed to look for a more welcoming place to catch the morning sunlight on her back.

Sarah rolled over on her stomach and pulled the quilt over her head. More noise. "Damn it! What the hell is that?"

Then she sat up and looked at the clock. It was 9 a.m. and she suddenly remembered that Patrick's work crew was here to replace the roof singles. She jumped up out of bed, put on her bathrobe and went into the bathroom to shower.

Haunted Heart / Laverne Stewart

As the warm water slid over her skin and she lathered her body with soap, she thought of all of the places Patrick's mouth and hands had been. She smiled. As she lingered in the warm water spray she thought about what a passionate and considerate lover he was. She'd not had too much experience but she knew what she liked and he was able to give it to her and then some.

Reluctantly she turned off the water and wrapped a towel around herself. Once she was dressed she went downstairs. She heard Hannah humming a happy-sounding tune. The melodic sound was coming from the kitchen. It wasn't a song she recognized but she thought it was very pretty. "What's that you're humming Hannah?"

"Well good morning to you girlie! That is an old Irish lullaby. It's one you should learn. You might be needing to know some tunes to hush a wee baby with."

Sarah made a face. "Don't start that again Hannah," Sarah said as she laughed and then looked into the oven. "What smells so good?"

"I am just baking sugar cookies and this pan is ready to come out of the oven. After you've had your breakfast why don't you take a plate of these and a pitcher of lemonade down to the men? I'm sure it's hot, dirty work they're doing fixing the roof and there's nothing they'd be wanting more than something to eat – and having it delivered by you will make it far more pleasing than seeing it brought by these old hands."

"Hannah I think you are in wonderful shape. And you do more than ten women that are half your age every day."

"Oh you think so do you? Well that might be so but I still say it's you who will be delivering this to the men for their break. Patrick was here very early. Why I got up at six a.m. and his truck was already parked out front."

Sarah didn't respond but her face turned a deep shade of crimson that spoke volumes.

Hannah said nothing as she turned her attention toward the dishes that were soaking in the sink. As she picked up a dishcloth she smiled to herself and thought of Evelyn Elizabeth. *"Yes now Evie, didn't I tell you things have a way of working themselves out. Give them some time and you will see that everything will be just fine. I know you've been waiting a long time but there will be a wedding sure enough."*

As soon as Sarah had finished breakfast she took the cookies and lemonade to the work crew that were standing by their trucks and sitting on the nearby grass of the front lawn. The men stopped talking as she made her approach.

"Good morning everyone! Hannah thought you might like a little something sweet on your break and she asked me to deliver it to you. Patrick I need to speak you when you have a moment."

"Yes Ms. Harrison."

She wasn't sure why he was being so formal with her but she didn't make any comment about it in front of his work crew. Instead she told them to enjoy the cookies and she made her way back into the house.

One of the men who was reclining on the grass let out a long, low whistle as soon as she was back inside. "Now there's a bit of sugar I wouldn't mind licking," the man said which resulted in howls of laughter from the other crew. Patrick glared at the man.

"Shut your mouth Murphy. That 'bit of sugar' as you call her is the new owner of this property and the one that's paying for this project. If you want to work here you'd best have a little bit more respect. Finish up what you're eating and get back to work all of you."

Patrick turned his back on the men and walked toward the house. He was surprised at how angry he felt in that moment and how fast he'd reacted to what Ron Murphy had said. He'd hired him five years ago when he started the company and had never yelled at him before. He knew the man could be crude at times and normally he wouldn't say anything about it because there wasn't a better roofer in the entire city and he was a fast worker too. But the way he looked at Sarah and that comment got under Patrick's skin. He would have to keep his distance from her around the workers. He didn't want them to know he was sleeping with the boss. And he thought *"What have you gotten yourself into Gallagher?"*

As Sarah went back inside she thought about Patrick's distance with her just then. Was he regretting their intimacy from the night before? She didn't. She never felt more alive and, while inexperienced in love-making, she was pretty sure no other man could make her feel the way he'd done the night before. Sarah reminded herself that there was so much she had to do. She needed to start going through the contents of the house. She'd decided that while she would keep some furniture there was simply too much to take back home to Boston with her. She knew many of the things in the home were very valuable and would be much sought after by antique collectors. It made sense to auction everything off that she didn't want. When she saw Patrick she would ask him which auction house he would hire.

Sarah spent the next couple of hours making an inventory of the contents of the basement. There wasn't much here of interest to her but she knew the old tools would likely be wanted by someone. By 1 p.m. Hannah was at the top of the stairs calling her name. "Come and have some lunch girlie before you faint from hunger."

Sarah had just eaten a few hours earlier and still wasn't hungry but she knew better than to argue with Hannah so she made her way upstairs. She opened the door and saw Patrick sitting at the kitchen table and Hannah at the sink filling glasses with water.

"Merciful Lord in heaven! Just look at you girlie! What were you doing down there? Go get yourself cleaned up before you sit down."

Patrick laughed out loud when he saw her. Sarah had no idea what was wrong until she caught a glimpse of herself in the mirror. Her face was smeared with dirt and there were cobwebs in her hair. She was indeed a sight and not a good one. She jumped in the shower and quickly washed off the grime. Then she changed her clothes and pulled her wet hair back into a ponytail. When she returned to the kitchen Patrick and Hannah were chatting and waiting for her to return before they ate.

"Come on and sit down before lunch goes cold girlie."

As usual everything was delicious and the few hours that she'd been working in the basement had helped give her a good appetite. As they were just finishing their meal Sarah asked about which auction house Hannah and Patrick thought had the best reputation in the city. They both agreed that it was Tim Isaac Auctioneers and then Patrick asked why she wanted to know about auction houses.

"Well I can't possibly take everything here with me back to Boston."

Patrick stared at Sarah and then quickly pushed his chair back from the table and got up.

"I see. Hannah, thanks for the wonderful lunch. Forgive me Ms. Harrison but if there's nothing else you need right now I must get back to work. You are not paying me to hang around and keep you company are you?"

Patrick turned his back on Sarah, walked out of the kitchen and went back to work.

"What's wrong with him?" Sarah asked aloud.

Hannah who was now clearing the dishes from the table was also annoyed. She hated to see Harrison House sold off one piece at a time but she had no right to voice her opinion about the future of the house and contents. She answered:

"Like me, Patrick has spent most of his life around this grand old place. It pains him to think that things are going to change. But change is a part of life and, if you decide to sell Harrison House and auction off the contents, that would be your business and not ours girlie."

 Hannah's words caught in her throat as she struggled to maintain her composure. She picked up dishes and carried them from the table to the sink. She kept her back to Sarah and continued to clean.

Sarah wasn't sure what to say or do so she left the kitchen and went to her room. She lay down on the bed and closed her eyes.

She didn't have the same deep emotional connection to the place that Hannah and Patrick did. But seeing how upset they were at the thought of the things here being auctioned off and the property being sold made her feel badly.

Haunted Heart / Laverne Stewart

But what was she supposed to do; hang on to this old mansion and live in it like old Gertrude Harrison?

Sarah had an image of herself in 50 years rambling around the massive home talking to herself and her cat. Just then Marmalade jumped up on the bed and started rubbing her face on Sarah's hand.

"That's not going to happen Fur Ball! I have plans for my life and they don't include this city, this mansion or all of the stuff that goes with it."

As if disgusted with her plans to sell the place and its contents Marmalade hissed and jumped off the bed. Sarah lay on the bed for a while longer. She decided that Patrick and Hannah would simply have to face facts. This place was going to be sold and she was going back to Boston as soon as it was ready to sell. But the work wasn't going to do itself and Sarah knew that if the house was going to be ready to show within the next few months she needed to get back to work. Sarah spent the rest of the day in the basement sorting though boxes and trunks. She'd sorted almost everything into three piles. One was trash, one contained things to sell and the other contained items she was going to keep. She got up from the floor where she'd been sitting sorting through things. Her muscles were sore. She needed a bath to ease them.

Sarah went up to her room and slipped out of the now filthy clothing she was wearing. She put on a bathrobe and went into the bathroom where she filled the tub with warm water and bubble bath. As she eased her body into the water she sighed and closed her eyes. She thought about Patrick and Hannah again. They were upset with her for wanting to sell the place and the things within.

What could she do? She couldn't keep it. It was far too large for just one person. And although it wasn't an exciting life she led in Boston, it was her life. She was determined to do what she had to do and move on.

She was tired. The long day of work, coupled with a night without much sleep, had left her exhausted. She closed her eyes. She knew she needed to smooth things over with Hannah and Patrick but she didn't know how to do this without giving up on her plan to sell the property. She needed to speak with Patrick. They'd avoided one another all day and she needed to know whether it was because he'd regretted the intimacy they had shared the night before or because she planned to sell everything. She needed to reassure Hannah that whatever happened to the house, she didn't need to worry about her apartment above the garage because she would make her remaining in it a stipulation of the sales agreement. She went downstairs to the first floor. The house was quiet. She entered the kitchen. Hannah wasn't here. There was a note on the table. *"Sarah, I left a plate in the refrigerator that you can warm up in the microwave. I am at my card club."*

It was after 7 p.m. but Sarah had no appetite. She went outside. There was no one around. All of Patrick's workers had gone home for the day. She was impressed with the progress they had made. She wondered whether Patrick would return this evening to consult with her about the house or whether he'd continue to keep his distance. Sarah went back inside. She found his business card in her purse. She picked up the phone in one of the parlors and dialed his cell phone number. It rang several times before it went to voicemail.

"Leave a message. I'll get back to you as soon as possible," the message said.

"Patrick, it's Sarah, I need to talk to you. If you get this message tonight please call or come over. Bye." Sarah hung up the phone.

"What do you want to talk about?" Patrick had come into the room as Sarah was leaving the message for him. She screamed.

"Don't sneak up on me like that!"

"I wasn't sneaking up on you. So, what is it that you want to talk about?" Patrick sat down on a sofa and crossed his arms over his chest.

Sarah stood in front of him. "Patrick I want to talk about why you are so upset with me. Was I really that bad in bed? You are acting as though nothing happened between us."

Patrick stood up and put his hand behind her head. He pulled her very close to him and lowered his head so that his mouth was inches away from hers. "How could I forget these lips?" He kissed her deeply and for a long time until she thought her legs would give out on her. "How could I forget this body and what you can do with it?" He ran his hands over her thighs and butt.

"Sarah you have turned me inside out. All I can do is think about wanting to be with you. But you are also my employer and I have signed a $100,000 contract to get this place restored in twelve weeks. How would it look to the guys on my crew if they knew I was sleeping with the boss? Talk about fringe benefits. When I am around them it has to be all business. When it's time to work it's time to work. But when it's time to play well, I am all yours Red."

Sarah understood the arrangement and agreed. This was a summertime fling anyway; nothing serious. When the house was ready to sell she would go her way and he would go his. Sarah also needed to talk to him about her plans to sell the house.

Haunted Heart / Laverne Stewart

"I understand that this place means more to you and Hannah than it does to me. It's been her home for fifty years and you've been coming here since you were a baby but you can't really expect me to keep this house Patrick. This mansion is huge. I have no intentions of living in it all alone like old Gertrude did."

Patrick looked deep into her eyes. "What if you found someone to share it with Sarah?" Patrick had dated many women over the years but he'd never considered the possibility of living with anyone until now. For a moment he pictured he and Sarah here together. The daydream ended when Sarah, who thought he was teasing, laughed.

"Why Patrick Gallagher the next thing you're going to say is 'Will you marry me and how many children do you want?' Come on we both know that what's happening between us isn't going to last. When the restoration is finished Patrick, I will go back to Boston and you will find another woman to seduce with that sexy-as-hell body and those killer blue eyes."

She took a step back from him and went to walk away but before she could he pulled her back into his arms which held her like a vice. His fingers became tangled in her hair and he kissed her. His tongue roughly explored her mouth and then he abruptly pulled away.

"If that's the way you want it Red. No problem. We'll keep this strictly recreational. I'll enjoy it. And when you decide you've had enough of me and this place we will shake hands and go our separate ways. Deal?"

Sarah straightened her shoulders and attempted to look as calm as he did. "Deal! Now if you'll excuse me I have lots of things to do. Goodnight Patrick!"

9

Sarah walked out of the room. She was determined not to show how shaken she was by the exchange. She practically ran up the stairs to her bedroom and slammed the heavy oak door.

Patrick stood there for a moment trying to gather his composure. He'd known many women but none of them managed to get under his skin like Red. That's how he thought of her now; Red. Red-hot. Hotter than any woman he'd never made love to before. What worried him was the very real likelihood of playing with this kind of fire and ending up getting burned. It was a risk he was willing to take.

Sarah spent the rest of the evening cataloging the contents of the library. This was a far bigger and more complicated job than she was capable of on her own. She decided she would need expertise help. In the morning she planned to call the New Brunswick Museum. She had wondered what she would do with all of the clothing and other items of no use to her but of great historic significance to the province. She thought likely the museum would be very interested in acquiring the things she had to donate.

In exchange for her donation she would suggest that the museum send over an expert to help go through all of the home's contents. Then, when she had catalogued everything and decided what she would keep and what she would sell, she would call Tim Isaac Auctioneers and have them collect the items she wished to have auctioned off.

Haunted Heart / Laverne Stewart

Old Gertrude was a bit of packrat who didn't believe in letting things go. More than 167 years worth of collectables and other treasures were here.

Then, her mind turned to the thought of how angry Patrick was with her and how disappointed she'd made Hannah. She could here her mother's voice again. *"What have you gotten yourself into this time Sarah?"*

"I don't know mother but I think I am in way over my head."

By 11 p.m. Sarah climbed the stairs and went into the bedroom where she slept. She looked out the window. Hannah's living room light was still on. She wondered whether Hannah would speak to her in the morning.

Sarah preferred to keep her distance from Patrick for the time being. Having a summertime romance with the contractor she'd hired to do an expensive renovation on this place was a stupid thing to do. There was no way it would end well.

Sarah didn't want to hurt Patrick and she didn't want to get hurt either. She would tell Patrick that last night had been a mistake and that she thought it best that they try to forget it had happened and keep things strictly business from now on.

To make sure she didn't risk getting caught up in the heat of the moment again, she would simply make sure she was never alone with him again.

She'd send him instructions through Hannah, she thought. That would be best for everyone. For the first time all day Sarah felt at ease.

Sarah slipped into a nightgown and climbed into bed. She was tired but she thought she would read more about Harrison House from the family biography.

After about half an hour she closed the book and turned off the light. She wondered how Evelyn Elizabeth's parents had coped with her death. She knew they'd been deeply religious. She wondered whether it brought them any comfort or whether they blamed God and the world for the loss of this beautiful girl.

Sarah closed her eyes and in a couple of minutes she was asleep. It wasn't long before she was dreaming once more...

Sarah was sitting at a desk in her bedroom. She was wearing a pale yellow dress that fell around her on the floor. She was dipping an old-fashioned quill pen in an ink well. She was writing in a leather bound book. It was a journal. She saw the words that she wrote:

April 3, 1847

"My dearest diary. Polly our cook and housekeeper isn't well today and has remained at home. So we are doing the cooking without any assistance today. Mother doesn't care to work in the kitchen so she has asked me to prepare father's dinner. As I was peeling vegetables and looking out the window to the back garden and the stables. I could see father talking to a most handsome young man. He is tall, with dark hair which is nearly as black as the horse he was holding steady by the reins. I saw father shake the man's hand and then they both walked into the stables together with the horse. When father came in for his dinner he told mother that he'd just acquired a new horse and that because it was young and needed some work he had hired a young horse trainer who will live above the stables with his younger brother and that he will care for the animal until it

is ready to be ridden. Mother asked why he'd purchased the horse because we already had several for the carriage and father's hunting stallion. I couldn't believe my ears when father said it was to be a present for my 16th birthday. Oh diary, she is the most beautiful creature in the world and I must confess to you dearest diary that the young horse trainer is also very appealing. This afternoon when father is freed from his work he has promised to take me to the stables to see my new horse and meet its trainer. I am thrilled beyond all description."

Next Sarah saw herself in the stable. She was petting the black filly on the nose and feeding it a carrot. She was laughing and talking to her father and the young horse trainer...

A sound of hammering was taking her attention. She was trying desperately to stay in the stables with the handsome young man. But the hammering sound continued. She opened her eyes. She was back from dreamland. The hammering was coming from outside.

Sarah looked at the clock. Once again she'd slept in. It was 9:30 am.

She got up and went to the bathroom. She jumped in the shower and washed her hair and her body. Her muscles were still a little sore from all of the work she'd done in the basement the day before so she remained under the hot spray for longer than she normally would.

Because she had forgotten to turn the bathroom fan on, the entire room was filled with steam. She wrapped a towel around her body and another around her hair.

She found a wide-toothed comb in her makeup bag and then began to comb out the wet curls.

Sarah went to wipe the steam from the mirror so she could see into it. On it someone had written the initials PRG.

She screamed and opened the door of the bathroom.

She ran to the bedroom and pulled on a pair of leggings and a T-shirt.

Within minutes Patrick was standing at her bedroom door.

"What's wrong Sarah? I could hear you screaming all the way outside."

"Come with me! She led him back into the bathroom where the steam had evaporated and the air, while still damp, was much clearer. Sarah pointed to the mirror. "Look!"

Patrick looked but didn't see anything to cause any alarm. "What's the problem?"

"I was having a shower and when I got out the room was filled with steam. The mirror was fogged over. I turned my back to wrap a towel around my self and when I turned around to wipe the steam from the mirror, the initials PRG were written there. Did you do this? If you did, I assure you I don't think it's funny!" Sarah was shaking and crying.

Patrick held her in his arms until she calmed down.

"Sarah I've been working outside for the past two hours. No one was in here except you. I know that's pretty strange but I promise you I didn't do it. Maybe you should talk to Hannah about it. I told you she is sensitive. She sees and hears things others don't. Maybe she will be able to help explain what happened. Are you okay? I have to get back to work. The roof is almost finished and I have a couple of the guys taking off some of the siding that's got dry rot. As soon as all of the siding is in order we'll scrape it and give it a fresh coat of paint. I expect we should be able to call in the landscapers as soon as we are finished with the outside house repairs which at this rate should be finished by the end of next week."

Patrick and Sarah looked at one another. Now neither were sure of what else to say.

"Umm yeah," Patrick finally said, "so I'm going back to work. Talk to you later."

"Okay, thanks." Sarah watched him descend the stairs.

The image of Padraig Gallagher's initials in the mirror had really shaken Sarah. She decided it must have been her imagination after the dream she'd had of Padraig and Evelyn Elizabeth.

Sarah decided to say no more about it. She pretended everything was wonderful as she walked into the kitchen where she found Hannah taking more cookies out of the oven.

"Lord above those young men have huge appetites," Hannah declared. "Patrick told me they couldn't get enough of the ones I sent down to them by you yesterday. So I thought I'd make them some more today. But this time it's gingersnaps."

Sarah had always loved Hannah's cookies when she was a kid and the gingersnaps were her favourite. She reached for one that Hannah had placed on a cooling rack. "Careful girlie, they're still hot. Take one from the biscuit tin and then take it down to the boys. Then you come back up here with me and we're going to have a little chat while you have your breakfast. Now there's a good girl, off you go."

Sarah went outside to the south end of the mansion where scaffolding had been erected and several men were removing old clapboard siding while others were installing new boards.

She marveled at how efficient the men worked together. There was little talk; after years of working together on many projects they knew exactly what they were doing so there wasn't a lot of need for conversation.

Sarah saw Patrick in the back garden talking to a man who held a clipboard in his hand. The man was nodding to something Patrick was saying.

Then the man made a hand gesture which told her that he was describing the work that needed to be done here. The man shook Patrick's hand and then got into a pick-up truck and drove away.

Patrick saw Sarah and waved before he walked up to her.

"Things look like they are coming along very well out here Patrick," Sarah said with a smile.

"Yup, they are. There was far less dry rot than I first anticipated. We should be finished replacing the siding by this evening. Tomorrow we'll start scraping off the old paint on the boards that don't need to be removed. I expect we'll get started on painting the place before the end of the week. Things are right on schedule."

Sarah looked at the house as she spoke to Patrick. It was easier to focus on the building and the workers than to look into his eyes. When he stared at her she was unnerved. She could tell what he was thinking and that bothered her. "Was that the landscaper you were talking to just a minute ago? When do you think the gardens will be finished?"

"Stan McLean is the guy I subcontract to do all landscaping jobs. He is very good and he always comes in right on budget and sometimes under. I told him he could get started at the far end of the property any time. He said he could be here the day after tomorrow. At this rate Sarah I think all of the exterior work will be done in a few weeks."

Patrick's stomach growled. He hadn't eaten breakfast. He looked at the container in Sarah's hands and recognized it to be one of Hannah's cookie tins. "Did Hannah happen to send something down for the morning coffee break?"

Sarah nodded. "May I?" Patrick took the tin from Sarah's hands and opened the lid. "Gingersnaps, yes!" he said with all of the enthusiasm of an eight-year-old boy. He reached into the tin and took a couple of the cookies out and took a bite out of one. "Yum. Delicious; still warm. Just the way I like them."

A couple of the guys who were nearby and heard Patrick talking about the cookies walked over with a look that said they all wanted to share in the delicious treat. One of them was Murphy the roofer. He reached for a cookie and looked at Sarah before he licked his lips and gave her a wink that told her he was interested in more than what was offering this morning. He smiled at her.

"How are you Ms. Harrison? Lovely morning isn't it? Almost and lovely as you I dare say."

Sarah felt uncomfortable around this man. He was too sure of himself. Something in the pit of her stomach told her to stay as far away from this guy as possible. She nodded at him but said nothing. Sarah didn't want to encourage a guy like him and she knew many men who came into the restaurant who reminded her of him. She had a feeling he thought he was God's gift to women and that they should consider themselves blessed to have caught his attention.

She turned back to Patrick. "Well if you will excuse me Patrick, Hannah is waiting to speak to me in the kitchen."

She turned and walked away but she was still within ear shot when she heard Patrick tell Murphy to watch his mouth and to get back to work. Sarah wasn't sure what had been said but she was pretty sure it was something filthy and it had been directed at her. "What a creep," she mumbled to herself as she went back inside.

When she returned to the kitchen she found Hannah placing a bowl of fresh fruit and yogurt on the table along with a bagel and a cup of tea.

"You must be half starved. Sit down girlie and eat this. I was just about to take a load off these old, tired feet of mine with a cup of Earl Grey."

Hannah poured the tea and then sat down beside Sarah. "So I thought someone had been murdered from the sound of all of the screaming you were doing this morning upstairs. I was just about to go up there and see what all the fuss was about when Patrick raced up the stairs ahead of me. I thought I'd leave everything up to him... So what was the trouble?"

Sarah explained that the long hot shower she'd taken had created a lot of steam and when she got out of the shower and had went to wipe the steam from the mirror so she could look into it to comb out her hair, she thought she saw the initials PRG in the mirror.

"But I am sure that was just my imagination because there is no possible way they just appeared on their own and I was all alone in the bathroom and the door had been locked."

"I see. Well girlie you can tell yourself you didn't see it but we both know that you did. And yes the door was locked but that didn't stop the sender of the message from putting those letters in the mirror."

Sarah had been sipping her tea and then put the cup down on the table. Some of the hot tea spilled on the tabletop because her hands were shaking. "Hannah how did those initials end up on the bathroom mirror?"

Hannah patted Sarah's hand and smiled. "Why Evelyn Elizabeth put them there of course."

10

Sarah looked at the old lady and stared. She had no idea what to say to this. Hannah had to be joking. It simply wasn't possible for a woman who'd been dead for 167 years to write on a fogged-up mirror.

"Now I know what you're thinking girlie," Hannah smiled, "but as sure as you and I are sitting here, Evelyn Elizabeth is with us in spirit. The spirits of the dead often hang around the places that they knew and loved. They do go to heaven but often they like to return to the places where they lived to check up on it or on the people who are now occupying their home. Our loved ones who cross over will check in on us all of the time to see how we are doing. They want to see how we are growing, if we are making good decisions, if we are following our dreams."

"If they know we are sad," Hannah continued, "they will come around to provide us with comfort. Our ancestors will even show up in times of celebration; a birthday, a holiday, a wedding, the birth of a baby. Spirits are not as they are made out to be in the movies. They are not scary or evil. They are beings of light and love. Our loved ones and ancestors who have crossed over are always trying to communicate with us but we overlook all of the signs. We over-think things. This is a natural, everyday, common thing girlie. Sometimes a spirit will manifest and appear before you but that takes a lot of effort on their part."

"Usually," she added, "you will feel their presence or they will send you signs such as a bird, a butterfly, a dragonfly or a cool breeze on your face. The more you acknowledge this Sarah the more often it will happen and the easier it will get and the stronger the communication with the other side and Evelyn will be for you. Sometimes someone dies suddenly or with unresolved issues. It is difficult for them to want to cross over to the other side. If they are frightened or sad, sometimes the living will feel those emotions too. It's not because they want to frighten you, they are simply trying to make you understand their story. When someone is a spiritual medium who has the ability to communicate with the dead and can speak to the spirit and explain their situation, often they are willing to cross over and go home to heaven. But if a spirit has unresolved issues they might refuse to go home until the matter has been dealt with."

Sarah wasn't sure she wanted to hear the answer but she asked anyway. "Is Evelyn Elizabeth haunting this place because she hasn't crossed over?"

Hannah shook her head. "No. She isn't stuck here. She and I had a talk many years ago and I explained to her that she was dead and that it was time to go home, which she did."

"So why is she hanging around here now? Is she my guardian angel?"

Hannah smiled and shook her head. "Of course not girlie; Evelyn Elizabeth was a person like you and I. People don't become angels when they die. Angels are direct expressions of the loving thoughts of God sent to watch over us and help us. They are with us before our conception, when we, too, are in soul form. They accompany us through birth and are with us in every thought, word and event we experience in life. Guardian Angels are committed to us for the entire journey of our life – they never leave us and we are their only occupation. They will be with us when we leave this life and when we are, again, a soul in heaven. Everyone has had at least two Guardian Angels and often more."

"So if Evelyn isn't an angel why is she hanging around?"

Hannah looked up but not directly at anything in particular. "Yes, I know Evelyn Elizabeth – I was just about to explain that. Hold on to your horses dearie"

Sarah's eyes grew wider. Was Hannah having a mental breakdown? She was talking to someone that wasn't there and that someone was, apparently her dead ancestor.

"Evelyn Elizabeth wants me to tell you that she is your spirit guide. A spirit guide is one who is now in spirit form but who once was a person just like you and I. Often these beings can be deceased loved ones, the souls of those you have never met in this lifetime or they can take the form of other creatures such as the eagle, the wolf or other things in nature, including butterflies and dragon flies. Evelyn Elizabeth has been watching over you since you were born. When you were a child you used to play with her. You might not remember this but it's so. I told you before you called her Evie. She kept you company in your room while your mother and father were busy with other things. You chose her to be your spirit guide and she remains with you watching over you throughout your life making sure that you are safe. She will never interfere with your life but she will gently guide you to your life's path and purpose. God created all of us with free will so of course it's up to you whether you choose to follow your destiny or take another path of your choosing. It's simply up to you girlie. Evelyn wants you to know that she's been trying to connect with you ever since you arrived here at Harrison House and she says she's not about to leave you alone until you listen to what she has to say to you. Believe me darlin' I have seen and heard and felt her enough times to know beyond a doubt that what I say is true."

She didn't want to insult Hannah but Sarah thought that the old woman was absolutely crazy. "This is too funny... Hannah you should call the TV show Medium and offer your services as a show consultant. This is great stuff for a Hollywood script writer."

"Believe what you want to believe Sarah but I'm telling you the truth. Evelyn Elizabeth is here to help you fulfill your life's purpose and she is one very determined spirit. Please listen to what she wants to say with an open heart and mind will you? Evelyn Elizabeth Harrison and Padraig Ryan Gallagher were madly in love. They had to keep their relationship a secret though because her parents would never have consented to a marriage between her and a horse trainer in their employment. They were ready to marry her off to someone who they considered more suitable. But Padraig and Evelyn knew they couldn't live without one another. She became pregnant and he went to her father to ask for his consent for them to marry. If they didn't receive his blessing they planned to elope. But the night he planned to ask for her hand in marriage something went horribly wrong and Padraig was killed. You have a destiny Sarah."

"Oh yeah – so what's my destiny?"

Just then Patrick walked into the kitchen and poured a glass of water and took a drink. Hannah looked at him. "He is."

Patrick leaned against the kitchen counter and gulped the water until it was drained from the glass. He poured a second glass. "I'm what?" he asked and then lifted the glass to his lips and drank some more.

Hannah looked at him and then at Sarah. "I told her that you are her destiny and sure enough she is yours."

Water spewed from Patrick's mouth as he started to choke. "Come again Hannah?"

Haunted Heart / Laverne Stewart

"You heard me – both of you. You are her destiny and she is yours. You are both meant to be together."

Patrick grinned and thought he'd have a bit of fun. He loved nothing better than to get a rise out of this woman who meant the world to him. "No Hannah. I think it's you who are my destiny. Marry me!" He picked her up in his arms and started to dance her across the kitchen floor as he sang the words of an old Lionel Ritchie song.

'Oh, you are my destiny
You are my one and only
You gave that joy to me
When my whole life was lonely
Angel in disguise
With your power of love
You just hypnotize
I just love the magic of your spell
How much joy we'll have together
Only time will tell'

"Put me down Patrick. Do you hear me boy-o! I said put me down this instant!"

Every day, every night
Oh, I know it's so right
When I see your face
Only time's gonna tell
But I know you so well
Girl, my love's for real

"Patrick Gallagher for the love of God and all of the saints in heaven put me down. I am getting dizzy with all of this twirling!"

Haunted Heart / Laverne Stewart

Patrick ignored Hannah's protests and kept on singing as he danced around the floor while he held her in his arms with her legs dangling a foot off the floor.

By now Hannah was laughing and soon Sarah joined her as she watched the spectacle that was happening before her.

Patrick tried to keep singing but he too couldn't keep from howling with laughter. He put the old lady back down on her feet. As soon as she had her balance she grabbed the tea towel on the counter and gave him a swat with it.

"You're a devil Patrick Gallagher; that's what you are. Now you get out of me kitchen before I take a wooden spoon to your arse!"

Patrick was wiping tears from his eyes from laughing hard. "Oh, no Hannah, not the wooden spoon again!"

"You might be the boss of those men but I'm in charge in this kitchen and don't think I'm too old or you're too big for me to do it. And I know your mother would tell me to give you a swat for her too with the way you carry on sometimes. Now you get back to work. And Sarah I am sure you can find something to do with yourself other than to sit there gawking and laughing!"

Sarah and Patrick ran out of the kitchen together like two misbehaving kids, laughing as they went.

Hannah who was trying hard to keep up the pretense of being angry chuckled to herself as soon as she was sure they were out of earshot. Then, she smiled and nodded at the invisible presence.

11

Sarah and Patrick both laughed as they walked down the hallway. They still were unsure of what to say to one another after the angry words they'd had earlier. By the time they reached the first parlor Patrick asked Sarah to sit down. He sat beside her on one of the sofas.

"Sarah, I'm sorry about yesterday. I know you have no ties to this place and you have every right to do whatever you want with it. I have no business to get upset. I guess I was a little overheated. Damn Red you do get under my skin." Patrick knew better than to do it but he couldn't help himself. He was looking at her lips and he needed to kiss them again. He leaned in and placed his lips against hers. He meant it to be gentle and conciliatory. But then Sarah sighed and opened her mouth allowing him to kiss her deeply and fully. In a few minutes he knew he wasn't going to be able to go back to work until the hunger that had been building inside of him for the past couple of days had been satisfied.

He stood up and took her hands and helped her up from the sofa. He picked her up in his arms and carried her to the third floor. He laid her on the bed. He locked the door and returned to her. They remained in one another's arms for the next two hours. Their lovemaking was tender and sweet as it always is between lovers after they've made up from an argument. Sarah snuggled into Patrick's chest

"Do you believe what Hannah says about the two of us being each other's destiny?"

Patrick raised himself up so that he could look into Sarah's eyes. "I don't know but I know one thing's for sure. You've been in my life for only a few days and nothing's the same any more. Sarah I know you want to sell this place and go home to Boston. I guess we shall see what's to be when that time comes. It will take until September before this place is ready for a real estate sign and until that time comes, I am willing to take whatever you want to give even if it is some work with benefits."

He kissed her again and then he looked at his watch. "Oh shit. It's almost 12:30. The guys will be wondering where I've been and so will Hannah. I bet she's got lunch ready. We'd better get cleaned up and get downstairs."

Sarah pulled on a bathrobe. "I will be down as soon as I've had a quick shower. Let's be very casual about this. I don't want Hannah knowing what we've been up to."

Patrick grinned like a naughty kid. "Sarah you need to understand something about our Hannah. She knows things and this is likely one of them."

Sarah's face reddened. "But we were very quiet. How does she know?"

"Beats me but ever since I was a little kid she always knew what I'd been up to. Don't worry Sarah. Hannah says we are one another's destiny. I am sure she is tickled pink that we were up here making love. Now if you can get showered and dressed and come downstairs without too much embarrassment, I will see you at the kitchen table for lunch."

Patrick pulled on his jeans and shirt. He kissed her once more and then swatted her behind as he whistled and walked out of her bedroom.

Sarah was conflicted. She loved the way he made her feel. He was everything she'd ever dreamed of in a man. But her life was in Boston.

She came to Saint John with the intension of selling this place and moving on with her life. But now there was a complication. That complication came in the form of a tall, ruggedly handsome man with dark hair and blue eyes.

She could hear her mother's words once more. "Sarah Jane Harrison you're looking for trouble and if you're not careful you're going to find it." Sarah sighed and smiled as she walked towards the bathroom. "Well mom looks like trouble found me."

If Hannah knew Patrick had been upstairs in Sarah's bedroom with her she didn't say a word about it. Instead she served lunch and the three of them talked about the restoration of Harrison House.

Sarah told them she'd decided that there were many things in the house that she would never use that should be donated to the New Brunswick Museum or Kings Landing, an historic settlement near Fredericton, which was about an hour north-west of Saint John.

"There are many steamer trunks and cedar chests with beautiful gowns and other garments that I am sure the museum would love to have for its collection," Hannah agreed. "Patrick you are on the board of directors at the museum; don't you think they'd accept this kind of donation?"

Patrick knew the museum's curator would be thrilled to have some of the things at Harrison House. They would be prized additions to its Victorian collection.

Sarah asked him whether, in exchange for the donations, the museum would be willing to help her catalogue everything in the house so she would know what she had and whether it was worth keeping, donating or auctioning.

"Garreth McGuire is the museum's curator. I have to call him this afternoon. I'll mention to him that you have things to donate to the museum and I will ask whether they have someone available to help you. There's a lot to go through Sarah. This could take weeks and lots of long hours and late nights."

Patrick had a plan but for the moment he thought he'd keep it to himself. *"This, he thought, is going to be fun."*

After lunch Patrick went back outside and continued to work with the men on the siding. No one questioned where he'd been. If they were curious about why he was inside so long they kept it to themselves. The work continued all afternoon. The sound of saws and an electric nail gun were very loud. Hannah had gone to the church to play cards and Sarah, who didn't think she could handle the noise any longer, thought she would go to a paint and wallpaper store at McAlister Place Mall. Every room needed to be brightened with a fresh coat of paint and period appropriate wallpaper. Sarah was well versed in Victorian décor from the many interior design classes she'd taken over the past several years. She knew she wanted to keep the décor as true to the mid 19th century as possible.

She knew that the choice of paint colors on the walls in Victorian homes was based on the use of the room. Walls that were in the entryways and stairs were painted a somber gray so they wouldn't compete with the surrounding rooms. Victorian society was also more male dominated, and the downstairs rooms were heavy and masculine in their style while the upstairs rooms were usually lighter and more feminine.

Haunted Heart / Laverne Stewart

Wallpaper was often made in elaborate floral patterns with primary colors in the backgrounds, such as red, blue and yellow and overprinted with colors of cream and tan. Flock papers were a favourite, especially red. Large scale patterns were used in large rooms with diagonal trellis patterns and stripes used to heighten low rooms while wavy stripes were deemed to be graceful. Small geometric patterns would hide soil in high traffic rooms such as sitting rooms, halls and stairs. Fresco papers, which still remained popular, had ornate columns and fanciful flowers.

Sarah knew that at that time they also liked depicting botanical themes with natural earth-tone colors because of their fascination with nature in shades of green, brown, red, and mustard. White was for painting woodwork, which would show up nicely against a colored wall.

Sarah spent a few hours with the store's in-house decorator going through wallpaper, books and paint samples. When she was finished she had selected all of the paper and paint that was needed for the job. She knew it was going to be expensive but she wanted to do this right and she didn't mind spending the money because she knew it would come back to her when the house was sold.

She arranged to have all of the many gallons of paint and rolls of paper delivered to the house when the time came for the work to be done.

When she was finished at the store she decided she'd go back to Harrison House and see what was going on. By now it was almost 5 pm. The work crew was just finishing up for the day when she arrived. They had made a lot of progress.

As men got into their trucks and pulled away she got out of her car and stood back to examine the restoration work that had been done so far.

Much had been accomplished this first week. Sarah made a mental inventory. The roof had been re-shingled and the siding was ready to be painted. At the far end of the property she noticed landscaping equipment had been brought on site to start the necessary work on the grounds. Sarah was satisfied. She knew that many construction projects tended to drag on for weeks because shady contractors were looking to take advantage of those who didn't realize the importance of contracts. This is why she'd specified a deadline to protect herself from a job crawling at a snail's pace and then having to pay for all of those additional labour costs. But she had insisted on a twelve week contract and Patrick had signed it so she knew that if he could help it the work would be finished on time.

She saw him talking to a few of the men who were packing up their trucks. She waved and then went into the house where she found Hannah in the kitchen humming to herself as she peeled vegetables.

"Well hello there. How was your afternoon girlie?"

Sarah told her about the paint and wallpaper she'd selected which pleased Hannah very much. She hated to see how the place had become so run down over the years and the thought of fresh paint and new vintage wallpaper made her smile. Hannah then told her about her afternoon of cards at the church.

It was nearly six o'clock and Hannah was just putting the final touches on supper as Patrick walked through the kitchen door and grinned. "I don't know what's more appealing, the smell of whatever is in the oven or the sight of the two prettiest women in Saint John.

Hannah flicked a dishtowel at him and chuckled. "Listen boy-o you don't need to come shining around me like that to get fed. I've already set a place at the table for you. Now go wash your hands. Supper will be on the table in two shakes of a wee lamb's tail."

Throughout the meal Hannah, Sarah and Patrick discussed how the exterior repairs were progressing. Sarah told Patrick about the paint and wallpaper she'd selected. He told her to be sure to use his contractor's billing number to take advantage of the discount he always received for large purchases at that store. Then Patrick told her that he'd spoken to the museum's curator who promised that he would send a volunteer to Harrison House tomorrow morning to help catalogue and sort through the home's contents.

"That's wonderful! It sure will go a lot faster if I have someone beside me through all of this who knows what they are doing," Sarah said.

Patrick didn't say anything but thought: *"Red I know exactly what I'm doing and you'll be surprised how much you're going to enjoy it."*

Sarah noticed Patrick smiling to himself and asked what was so funny. "Nothing. Great supper Hannah," he said as he stood up and kissed the old lady on her cheek. I've got to run. Ma needs some help down at the church hall to get ready for the dinner and dance tomorrow night."

Hannah had been thinking this would be a great opportunity to get Patrick and Sarah to spend more time together away from the house.

"That's right Patrick I'm going there too. The tables have to be set up and the hall needs to be decorated. Why don't you come along Sarah? It's our annual fundraising dinner and dance that we hold to help the church with its financial needs. Years ago more people went to church and helped it with expenses. Now it takes this and things like dinners and bingo to keep the doors open. We can always use another set of hands and you'll be able to meet Patrick's Mother. Hannah noticed the time. "Good God in heaven where's the time gone? I promised your Ma I'd be there at seven o'clock and here it is six-thirty. I'll never get the kitchen cleaned up and be there on time."

Sarah and Patrick insisted that if she allowed them to help they would be able to be there on time. True to their word the kitchen was clean and they were on their way to St. Anthony's church hall 20 minutes later. When they arrived they found about a dozen parishioners setting up tables and chairs and decorating the entire hall.

Patrick's mother Eileen Gallagher was placing plastic table cloths and vases with plastic flowers on the tables. As small and wiry as Hannah was Patrick's mother was large. The hall was very warm and her flushed face told just how uncomfortable she was in it. "Merciful God above but it's warm in here," she said as she laughed and wiped the beads of sweat from her forehead.

Patrick came up behind her and grabbed her around the waist. "Guess who good looking?"

"Patrick Gallagher quit that nonsense and go do something," Eileen Gallagher said with a laugh. "We've got a lot of work to do here before tomorrow night and that kind of Tom foolery isn't going to make it happen any faster."

"Sure Ma but I want to introduce you to Sarah Harrison."

Sarah extended her hand which Eileen grabbed and pulled her close before she gave her a big hug. "So you're the pretty thing that's taking my boy's time and attention these days. Well Hannah likes you awful well. Anyone who has her approval is in my good books too. It's so good of you to come help us here. We've got a lot left to do. I hope you'll come to the dinner and dance tomorrow night. Patrick can pick you and Hannah up and then get me and we can all come together. Okay, now that that's settled you can help me set the tables. Patrick I need you to climb the ladder and string the white lights through the rafters. Okay now off with you boy. Sarah and I are going to get to know one another a little better."

By 11 p.m. the hall had been transformed into a summer garden. When Patrick finished stringing the white lights and turned them on the place looked even more romantic. Everyone was tired and it was time to go home. Eileen Gallagher had come to the church with one of the other widows. Patrick offered to drive his mother home before he dropped Hannah and Sarah off at Harrison House. The older ladies chatted all the way to Eileen's home. Patrick got out of the truck and opened his mother's door before he walked her to front porch and kissed her goodnight.

Hannah and Sarah, who were sitting in the truck's back seat watched. "Patrick and his mother are very close. Liam Gallagher, Patrick's father, died when he was a boy. It was an industrial accident at the port where he was a longshoreman. Eileen never got over it and refused to consider any other man. Patrick is a good son. He looks out for her.

As busy as he is with all of his work he always makes time for his mother. A man that's good to his Ma is also someone you could count on in marriage too."

Sarah wondered why Patrick wasn't already married. At 35 she was sure, as handsome as he was, there had to have been plenty of opportunities and many women who'd be very eager to fill the role of his wife. She knew beyond a doubt that he wasn't gay. So why wasn't he married or living with someone? She never voiced her thoughts aloud but Hannah answered her questions anyway.

"Yes that boy is as good looking as the day is long that's for sure. He's had a lot of girls but no serious relationships. He's always been too busy studying and running his construction business. It would have to take someone pretty special to turn his head towards marriage I would dare say. He seems to be very taken with you girlie."

Sarah was about to protest when Patrick jumped back in the truck and they were off to Harrison House.

When they arrived at Harrison House it was 11:30 p.m. Patrick and Sarah walked Hannah up to her apartment door. Sarah gave her a hug and Patrick kissed her on the cheek and they said goodnight.

Patrick then walked Sarah to the door and said goodnight to her too.

"Aren't you coming in?" Sarah asked.

"We were up most of the night. I need some sleep and so do you. I know if I go inside with you we'll just have another all-nighter. Not that I wouldn't love anything better. But you've got a busy day tomorrow. The volunteer from the museum will arrive early tomorrow to help you get started so you need your rest. Good night Sarah." Patrick's kiss was so passionate Sarah felt her legs weaken and her stomach quiver. He grinned and winked.

"I do believe I have found the secret to having the last word with you Red. I just need to kiss you into submission and silence. I'll talk to you tomorrow. Let me know how you are getting along with the guy from the museum."

12

Sarah's mind was rattled after that kiss and all she managed to do was smile and wave as she went into the house and locked the front door.

She went upstairs and changed into her white cotton nightgown, brushed her teeth and slipped between the cool cotton sheets on her bed. In minutes the fatigue she was feeling sent her into a very deep and sound sleep.

She awoke the next morning with the sun in her eyes and the sound of the doorbell ringing in her ears. She jumped out of bed and looked at the clock. She'd slept in again. She pulled on a bathrobe and raced down the stairs in time to see Hannah heading for the front door.

"Go get yourself dressed Sarah. I'll give him a cup of coffee and talk to him until you're ready."

Sarah raced back up the stairs and quickly showered and changed into a pair of jeans and a sweatshirt. When she entered the kitchen she saw Patrick sitting at the table sipping coffee and eating a muffin. "Patrick what are you doing here this early?"

"You wanted some help sorting through all of the stuff in this place."

"The museum volunteer is going to help me with that. You don't have to bother with this on your day off. It's the weekend."

Patrick grinned at her and tipped his hat. "Sarah, I *am* the museum volunteer and this is something I like to do on my days off. Whenever you're ready, I am."

Sarah had a cup of coffee and a muffin with Patrick and Hannah. They decided they'd go through everything in the attic first. As they left the kitchen Hannah smiled and looked across the table at an empty chair.

"That man is falling for her, of that I have no doubt. The more time they spend together she will discover that she too is in love with him. There'll be a wedding here before the leaves fall from the trees don't you think Evelyn?"

Due to the morning air was cool, the attic wasn't too warm. Patrick opened the windows on either side of the attic to allow a cross breeze and some fresh air. They started opening trunks.

Patrick had brought with him a record book and donation forms for every item that Sarah chose to donate to the New Brunswick Museum. Every item she decided to donate would be catalogued and packed into containers before they were taken to the museum where antiquities experts would further evaluate them.

As they started to open the first two of what were more than a dozen steamer trunks and cedar chests, Patrick told Sarah that he'd been a volunteer at the museum ever since he'd been a graduate student working on his PhD in Maritime history.

Patrick explained that the province's architecture and handcrafted furniture and other goods of the 1800s were a couple of his passions.

"When I told the curator that you wanted to donate some of the things here to the museum he was really excited.

Haunted Heart / Laverne Stewart

Museums rely on the generosity of others to build their collections. Some museums have a budget for acquisitions and in these economic times, more museums than ever before really depend on donations such as this. The museum's collection of clothing worn by someone who lived in this city in the 1800s will be a wonderful addition. In fact, anything in this house you choose to donate to the museum would be a real treasure because the things here really tell the story of life in this city at that time. Some museums focus on a broad topic instead of a regional history approach. The New Brunswick Museum is dedicated to telling the history of this province, its culture and the people who once lived here. This house, Sarah, is a living museum. What we are sorting through today will go to experts who specialize in 19th century textiles. If you choose to donate any furniture it will be examined by those people who have expertise in furnishings. The more information we can provide the museum about your objects the better. Museums are interested in biographical information about the person who made or used the object, where it was purchased, how old it is, and what modifications or repairs have been made to it. Anything you can tell the museum about your donation will be helpful in documenting the object's history," Patrick explained as he looked into a trunk that had a brass plate on it with the name Evelyn Elizabeth Harrison.

"See this is good. Right away we know that the contents of this trunk belonged to your ancestor Evelyn Harrison. We know she died when she was 16. It looks like these things are in excellent condition. Someone took the time to pack them with mothballs which has kept them from being destroyed by insects and mould."

They went through the first two trunks that were filled with gowns. Sarah couldn't see any reason why she would want to keep any of it. She signed the official document called a

Haunted Heart / Laverne Stewart

Deed of Gift that transferred ownership of the dresses from her to the museum which meant that it now became the property of the museum in perpetuity.

"Are you sure that you want to donate these items Sarah? Once the Deed of Gift, which is a legally binding contract has been signed, all of these donations cannot be returned to you."

"I'm sure. I like vintage clothing but I think this is taking vintage a little too far. Can you see me wearing one of these to the dance tonight?" Sarah held Evelyn Elizabeth's pink gown up to her and twirled around the floor.

Patrick stood up and took the gown from her and placed it in a museum container. "Actually I've been picturing you absolutely naked and in my bed since I left you last night. Maybe after the dance we will have to turn that fantasy into reality," he said as he kissed her.

When he let her go, she caught her breath and smiled. "Maybe, we'll see, but we have a lot of work to do up here today and we are never going to get to it if you do that anymore."

Patrick smiled and then assured Sarah that she would be entitled to a tax deduction for the appraisal value of her donation. This, he explained, would come in handy with the inheiritace tax she would have to pay on the property.

As they continued to go through trunks and cedar chests Patrick told her a little bit about the museum's history.

"It's the oldest continuing museum in the country and was officially incorporated as the Provincial Museum in 1929. The next year it was named the New Brunswick Museum. In 1934 it was located just down the street from here on Douglas Avenue and it was officially opened by Prime

Haunted Heart / Laverne Stewart

Minister R.B. Bennett. As of 1942, the collections, building and properties of the museum officially became the property of the people of New Brunswick. Today the museum is a provincial institution and is funded by the provincial government. It continues to collect, preserve, study and exhibit our natural and cultural heritage. This is why everything you are donating is so important, Sarah. It also has a remarkable natural sciences collection with one of the largest collections of 19th century decorative arts and Canadiana in the Atlantic Provinces."

Patrick explained that in 1992 the museum outgrew its space on Douglas Avenue and plans were made to develop new exhibition galleries in the central part of the city. Four years later the New Brunswick Museum officially opened its doors at Market Square in what was a former shopping mall in uptown Saint John.

While the exhibition centre covers three floors and 60,000 square feet; the collection centre, archives, research library and head office are still at the Douglas Avenue location.

"You really know a lot about the museum and this city's history don't you Patrick?"

Patrick smiled and shrugged. "Like I said it's one of my passions. Want to know what my other passion is?" He walked over to her and wrapped his arms around her and whispered in her ear. "I am absolutely passionate about making love to a certain long-legged red head with the most gorgeous body and face I have ever seen."

Sarah laughed and pushed him away. "Get back to work Gallagher."

"Sure thing, Red. You're the boss."

After four hours they had managed to go through most of the 12 trunks in the attic. Sarah decided to donate all of what was here as it was mostly clothing, shoes and other items she had no use for. Patrick's stomach was growling loudly. They both laughed.

"I might be the boss of this restoration project but your stomach sounds like it's in charge of your body. I think we'd better get something to satisfy it now."

Patrick couldn't help but flirt with her. "Red you are definitely the boss of this body and the only thing that will satisfy it is to have a close encounter with yours. But yeah, I am starving. Let's get out of here for a while."

They went downstairs and found a note from Hannah who'd written that she was out for the rest of the day and that they'd have to fend for themselves for lunch. Patrick suggested that they go to his favourite restaurant in the city. It was an Italian place called Vito's that served the best Chicken Ceasar salad and lasagna he'd ever eaten. It was 1 p.m. and Sarah realized that she too was very hungry.

They drove from Douglas Avenue to Germain Street and pulled up in front of an old brownstone building that reminded Sarah very much of some of the buildings in Boston.

Patrick got out of the truck and walked around to the other side where he opened her door and helped her down from her seat. Then he opened the restaurant's door and invited her to go inside. Usually crowded, the popular restaurant was less so. The hostess seated them at a corner table before she lit a candle and told them their server would be with them momentarily. The young man, whose nametag said Guido, came by their table and asked if they would like something from the bar. Patrick ordered a beer and Sarah said she would like a glass of the red house wine.

Over the next two hours they ate and talked. Patrick told her more about his childhood and she explained what it was like growing up in Boston. The food, as promised, was delicious. She had eaten a lot of great Italian food in Boston but it didn't come close to what was served here.

When Guido returned to clear their plates, he asked if either of them wanted to have dessert. Sarah placed a hand on her stomach and said she was absolutely too full to even think about it. Patrick however had room for more and ordered a slice of the restaurant's signature double chocolate cheesecake with two forks. "You really have to try it Sarah. Just one bite and you'll be addicted. I guarantee it."

When it arrived Patrick put a bite of the cheesecake on his fork. "Now be a good girl and open your mouth. I promise you are going to love what I have for you."

Sarah couldn't miss the double meaning and blushed which made Patrick laugh out loud. She closed her eyes and savoured the delicious offering. "Ummm," she said as she kept her eyes shut enjoying the delectable dessert.

Patrick handed her the fork and said "I dare you not to take a second bite. It is irresistible. It is almost as good as sex. Not quite but almost as good. Definitely not as good as sex with me," he said as he put a forkful of the cheesecake in his mouth and winked."

By 3:30 pm the meal was over and they left the restaurant. They returned to Harrison House where they agreed to go back to work for another couple of hours and then they'd get ready for the dinner and dance.

"Dinner's in another three hours. I am not going to be able to eat until tomorrow I'm so full."

Sarah put the key in the lock and opened the front door. They walked inside and Sarah walked ahead of Patrick as they climbed the stairs to the attic. Patrick enjoyed the view. Her jeans hugged her in all the right places he thought to himself. Over the next two hours they'd finished cataloguing and packing items into the museum's containers. Tomorrow Patrick would arrange for a truck to come to pick them up to be delivered. He looked at his watch. It was 5:30 pm.

"We have to leave in an hour. I don't have time to go back to my apartment. I brought a change of clothing with me this morning in case we got dirty up here. Do you mind if I shower and dress here?"

They went down to the third floor where they both went to separate bathrooms to bathe and dress for the dinner and dance.

By the time Sarah was ready she came downstairs where she found Hannah and Patrick waiting for her in one of the parlors. Patrick looked incredibly handsome in dark jeans and a crisp white cotton shirt that showed off his dark complexion and sapphire blue eyes. Patrick whistled out loud when he saw Sarah in a pink sleeveless dress and heels.

"Am I overdressed?"

"You're perfect. Then he turned to Hannah and said "All of the men at the church hall will be jealous of me. I'm going to walk in with two hot babes on my arms."

Hannah looked at her watch. "Patrick will you stop your flirting and let's go. I told your mother we'd pick her up at 6:15 and if we don't leave now we're going to be late and you know how your mother hates to be late."

Haunted Heart / Laverne Stewart

They arrived at the church just before 6:30 p.m. The hall was filled. She estimated there must be well over 100 people who were waiting in line to help themselves to the platters of meats, cheeses, salads and more that filled two long tables.

Sarah was still full from lunch but she didn't want to offend the Catholic Women's League members including Eileen and Hannah who'd made the food, so she took a little bit of salad and a couple of slices of ham.

They made their way to a table where several others were already seated. Hannah and Eileen introduced Sarah to everyone who smiled and made her feel welcome.

Across the room Sarah saw someone she thought she recognized. Then the man looked up and noticed her too. He smiled. It was Murphy the roofer. He continued to stare at her.

Sarah felt uncomfortable and looked away. She then tried to focus on the conversation that was happening at the table. However she had an uneasy feeling. She made a decision to avoid him if at all possible.

After the food had been cleared away, the tables were pushed back toward the walls to make room for people to dance in the centre of the hall. The florescent lights were shut off and the white sparkling lights that Patrick had strung through the rafters had been illuminated. It made the hall look like a romantic summer garden at night.

The music started to play and couples went to the dance floor. Hannah and Eileen remained seated talking and laughing with a group of other women their age.

Patrick got up from his chair and asked Sarah to join him in a waltz. The music was soft and slow.

Sarah wasn't a good dancer but she could tell Patrick was and in his arms she felt good as they made their way around the floor with the other couples.

When the dance was over Patrick asked if he could get her something cold to drink. He had only just arrived at the punch table when Murphy made his move.

"Hey there… do ya wanna have a dance?" He stunk of stale beer. This was a church hall and liquor wasn't allowed at this dinner and dance. He looked as though he'd been drinking for a while.

"No thank you Mr. Murphy. I am here with Patrick Gallagher and he's just gone to get me something to drink. He'll be right back."

"S-s-suit yourself but you don't n-n-know what you're missing."

Murphy snorted in disgust and then he stumbled and walked away.

Hannah had noticed Murphy. "That kid's got no manners. Just like his grandfather. All of those Murphy's think they're God's gift to women. You did the right thing Sarah. He'd have been all over you like a cheap suit if you'd have said yes. Be careful of that one Sarah," Hannah said.

By now Patrick had returned with punch for Sarah, Hannah and his mother. "Be careful of who Hannah?"

"I was telling Sarah to stay clear of Ron Murphy. He's trouble."

Patrick looked across the hall to where he'd seen Murphy sitting earlier in the evening. He wasn't there. "Did he do something or say something to you Sarah? Do you want me to find him and straighten him out?"

Sarah didn't want to ruin everyone's evening and she insisted that she was fine, that there was nothing to worry about because nothing had happened. Just then an old Faith Hill and Tim McGraw song called *It's Your Love* started to play and Sarah asked Patrick to join her on the dance floor.

They continued to enjoy the evening until the lights came up at midnight and it was time to go.

Patrick drove his mother home first and then, as they did the night before, walked Hannah to her apartment above the garage. Patrick walked Sarah up to the front door. He wanted to come inside but he was waiting for an invitation. He didn't have to wait long. Sarah reached up and put her arms around his neck and stood on her tiptoes to kiss him.

"I thought we might take some more inventory of what I've got up in my bedroom," she said and kissed him again.

Patrick groaned. "If that's what you have in mind that's likely going to take most of the night. Okay I'm all yours."

Just then, Patrick's cell phone rang. It was his mother. He listened to what his mother said and then he assured her that he would return to her house.

"Mom says she went to make herself a cup of herbal tea before bed and she blew a kitchen fuse. The lights are out and she can't see to find the breaker. I'll be back as soon as I can." He kissed her and then ran to his truck.

Sarah stood on the front steps and watched Patrick drive off. What she didn't know was that Murphy had been watching them. Just as she turned her back and walked inside he sprang from his hiding place and tackled her!

Haunted Heart / Laverne Stewart

13

Murphy fell on top of her. His sour, stinking breath was even more foul than it had been earlier that evening.

"I've been watching you all week Sarah. I've been thinking about that tight ass and those lovely tits of yours. Thought I'd drop by to see if you are really as hot as you appear to be. Gallagher left you here all alone. Why don't you and me keep each other company tonight?"

He slipped his tongue into her mouth and then slipped a hand under her dress that was now up around her thighs. Sarah was screaming and struggling to get Murphy off her. She managed to free one hand. She dug her fingernails into his skin and drew blood. He howled and then slapped her across the face.

"Bitch! So that's how you like it eh? Rough? Well I can do rough. Now you behave and I promise I won't leave too many bruises. Hell you might be begging me not to stop when I get through with you."

Sarah was screaming loudly enough that neither she nor Murphy heard the door open. A hand reached out and grabbed Murphy by the back of the shirt and lifted him from the floor. It was Patrick. His fist flew and struck Murphy between the eyes. Blood flew from his nose which was now visibly broken. Murphy fell to the floor. He was out cold. Patrick then helped Sarah to her feet. She was shivering and sobbing in his arms. He could see in the dim light that her lip had been split. "There now, Sarah, it's okay. I'm here."

Patrick picked up his cell phone and called 9-1-1. After he was assured that the police were on their way he called his mother. "Ma, yeah, I know. I was on my way over but there's a bit of a problem over at Harrison House and I have to stay here. I am going to call your neighbour Jim. He will help you out. I'll call you in the morning."

As they waited for the police to arrive Patrick held Sarah in his arms while he kept watch over Murphy to make sure he didn't get away. "Thank God I turned around."

"Why did you?"

"I don't know really. I only drove a few blocks when I knew I just had to turn around. Whatever the reason it's a good thing I did. I'd hate to think what would have happened if I'd driven over to Ma's house and left you here with that bastard."

Just then the police cruiser pulled up. Two officers got out of their vehicle and walked up to the front doors. Patrick let them in. They handcuffed Murphy and placed him in the patrol car and then took statements from both Sarah and Patrick. They promised someone would be in touch with them tomorrow.

Patrick took Sarah inside. He washed the blood from her swollen lip and then helped her upstairs to her bedroom. He helped her out of her dress and into a cotton nightgown and then helped her into bed.

He slipped out of his shirt and jeans and then slipped into bed beside her. For the rest of the night he held her tightly. The last words he said and those she heard before they both fell asleep were "Don't worry Sarah, I'm right here. You're safe. I'm not leaving you."

Sunday morning. There was nothing that had to be done that couldn't wait a while. Patrick woke early and was careful to slip quietly out of bed so he didn't wake Sarah. He dressed and went downstairs. Hannah was just making coffee when he walked into the kitchen.

"Patrick you're here early. Or did you stay the night?"

Hannah took a deep breath and her arms instinctively folded over the chest and she hugged herself as Patrick recounted what had happened to Sarah the night before.

"That bastard hit her in the mouth and split her lip. I came in just as he was putting his hand up under her dress. I want to kill him!"

Hannah put her hand on Patrick's arm and looked up into his eyes.

"There now boy-o you'll do nothing of the sort. The police and the courts will take care of the likes of him. You need to concentrate on helping Sarah get over that what's been done to her. You need to be kind and gentle now. I know you and she have been romantic with one another but you'll need to be forgetting all of that for a while. Sarah doesn't want or need sexual advances now. She needs to know that she is safe. You stay away from her until she is ready and comes to you. Do you hear me boy-o? I'm going to go into the herb garden and find what I'll need to help her with that cut lip. I'd guess if he tackled her to the ground she's bruised and sore too. You take some chamomile tea up to her and stay there until I come up to see what that monster did to the poor wee lamb."

Patrick boiled the tea kettle and made the herbal tea as Hannah had instructed. He carried it up to her room and as he placed the cup on her bedside table she woke. Her mouth was bruised, swollen and her lower lip was indeed split. He sat on the edge of the bed. With a gentle hand he touched her hair and asked how she was feeling.

"I feel really stupid. I don't think I did anything to make him think I was interested in him."

"You can't blame yourself. You didn't do anything wrong Sarah. Murphy's a dog. He always has been. He'll be going to jail for this Sarah and when he's free he'll never work in this city again. I'm going to make sure of that."

Just then Hannah arrived. "Oh my dear girl let me look at you. What did that monster do to you? Patrick you leave us now. I want to speak to Sarah alone. Go have a cup of coffee and after a while I'll come down and get your breakfast for you."

Patrick excused himself and Hannah sat on the bed close to Sarah and leaned down to examine her face. Sarah looked up into the old lady's wrinkled face and started to cry. Hannah took Sarah into her arms and held her until she stopped crying.

"There now girlie you let it all out now. There, there girlie. It's going to be okay. That man's not going to hurt you again. Now you let old Hannah have a look at that cut on your lip."

Sarah stopped crying and laid back against the pillows as Hannah examined the cut and bruises on her face.

"I've made a tincture of myrrh and water. This is an herb I use to clean wounds and help prevent infections. Now we'll just dab the myrrh mixture onto your lip and allow it to air dry. You be sure to use this twice a day. I've also brought you some aloe gel from the aloe plant in my kitchen. This is wonderful to help heal cuts and it will reduce the chance you will have a scar. It's a natural anti-inflammatory agent which should help take away the swelling," she said as she dabbed some aloe on Sarah's skin.

"It also helps new tissue to grow so the cut on your mouth will heal faster. Are you sore dearie? I have an essential oil with something called arnica in it. This has pain-relieving, antiseptic and anti-inflammatory properties and will help with any bruises you might have. You simply apply the arnica oil to the bruised skin several times a day." This is lavender oil," she said as she put a few drops on her fingertips and massaged Sarah's temples with it. "It helps to get rid of headaches and helps you to relax."

Next she handed Sarah the cup. It's chamomile tea; one of my favorite herbs for pain relief. You drink it all now, you hear? It should help if you are sore. Marjoram and rosemary and echinacea are also great for muscle and joint pain. I've brought you these essential oils too. If you want I will massage them into your skin and they will help take away any body aches you might have. Now would you like me to bring your breakfast up to you dear?"

Sarah thanked Hannah for her kindness but wasn't sure she was comfortable with having the oils applied to her skin. "Do you mind if we don't bother with breakfast or the massage Hannah? I think I just want to sleep some more."

"Sure enough girlie. You've been through a lot; that you have. I'll close the drapes so the sun's not in your eyes. You sleep now and I'll be up to check on you later."

Marmalade walked into the room just before Hannah had closed the bedroom door. As Hannah pulled the covers up to her chin, Marmalade jumped up on the bed and settled herself near Sarah's pillow and started to purr. It was as though the cat knew Sarah felt vulnerable and needed to be watched and cared for.

Haunted Heart / Laverne Stewart

"What do you want fur ball?" Sarah asked the orange cat as she scratched her under the chin. "You here to keep me company? Okay, you can stay but keep it down."

Sarah rolled over on her side and closed her eyes. It wasn't long before she was dreaming again. And in her dreams she wasn't alone. *Evelyn Elizabeth Harrison walked into her room and sat on the edge of her bed. She smiled.*

"Hello Sarah. You're hurt but it could have been worse. I sent Patrick to rescue you and he did. He loves you Sarah and I do believe you are falling in love with him too. He is a good man. So was my Padraig. Those Gallagher boys are handsome are they not? Patrick says he will never leave you. I wish for you a life time of happiness. That is something that Padraig and I never had. You and he are one another's destinies. Let it happen Sarah and you will never regret it."

Sarah slept for several more hours. When she woke her whole body ached. Slowly she got out of bed. She decided a soak in the bathtub with some Epsom salts would help ease the soreness. She ran the tub and then looked in the mirror. Her lips were swollen and cut. There was a nasty purple bruise on her cheek where he'd struck her with his fist.

"Well aren't you beautiful," she said. Sarah wasn't one to feel sorry for herself. She learned early in life it was better to swallow sadness and disappointment like a bitter pill and get on with life. She decided as soon as she wasn't feeling like she'd been run over by a train she'd get busy with getting the house ready to sell and then she'd drive back to Boston as soon as the sale sign was on the front lawn.

She simply wouldn't allow herself to dwell on that monster for that's what he was. No one who had an ounce of decency would hurt someone in this way.

Sarah kept her thoughts to the things that needed to be done at Harrison House. When the water started to cool she eased her body out of it and dried herself off with a towel. The Epsom salts had helped a little. Perhaps she would take some of Hannah's herbal teas and essential oils too; anything to feel like herself again, she thought.

She dressed and then went down to the kitchen where she found Hannah doing a crossword puzzle.

"What are you doing out of bed? You need to rest yourself after what you've been through girlie."

Sarah shook her head and then smiled. "No Hannah what I need is a cup of your herbal tea and as soon as I don't feel as sore I'm getting right back to work. I have decided not to think about last night any more. Well, I won't think about it until I have to. I suppose I will have to deal with this when he is charged and I have to appear in court."

Just then the phone rang. Hannah got up from her chair to answer it. "Harrison House. May I help you? Yes, she's here. One moment please." Hannah passed the phone to Sarah. "It's a Detective Bill Carruthers for you."

Sarah took the phone from Hannah. Her hand was shaking. "Hello? Yes, this is Sarah Harrison." Sarah listened to the police officer and then said thank you and goodbye.

"Detective Carruthers wants to come by in a little while. He says he has some news about the case and that he'd rather tell me in person," Sarah said softly.

Hannah knew even before the phone the call had ended. Young Murphy was dead. He'd been literally scared to death.

Haunted Heart / Laverne Stewart

14

It was just before 4 p.m. when Detective Carruthers arrived.

Sarah asked Hannah and Patrick to stay with her to hear the news and the police officer had no objections.

The four of them sat in the front parlor. Hannah had made tea and poured it for all of them before she sat on the sofa next to Sarah. She placed her hand on Sarah's arm.

Patrick sat in a chair beside the fireplace. He wasn't sure what was happening but he knew it couldn't be good.

The detective took a sip of the tea and then asked Sarah how she was feeling.

"I'm a little bruised and sore but otherwise I'm fine."

"Ms. Harrison I have some news about Mr. Murphy. After he was arrested last night he was taken to a holding cell where he was held overnight. He was supposed to remain there on a 48-hour remand until Monday morning when he was to be charged for the sexual assault against you. That's not going to happen now."

Patrick stood up. "And just why the hell not? Look at what that bastard did to this woman. Don't tell me. Let me guess. You cops screwed up when you booked him and he had to be released on some technicality?"

The officer ignored the remark and asked Patrick to have a seat and remain calm so he could explain what had happened.

Haunted Heart / Laverne Stewart

"Around three-thirty a.m. screams were heard coming from Mr. Murphy's cell," Detective Curruthers began. "The on-duty officer went to check on him and found him on the floor. He was holding his left arm and was visibly in distress. He appeared to be suffering a heart attack. The officer radioed for help and started to administer CPR. An ambulance took him from the holding cell to the emergency room at Saint John Regional Hospital. The attending physician said he'd indeed had a massive heart attack which was the cause of his death at five-forty-nine this morning."

"A heart attack? But Murphy was only 36 years old and he was very fit. How in the hell could he have had a massive heart attack?" Patrick wondered aloud.

"All the report says is that he was screaming and yelling for someone to protect him from something or someone he said was with him in the cell and that he was frightened. The guard thought that Murphy was undergoing an alcohol induced hallucination and didn't pay too much attention at first. He stated that Murphy kept begging her to go away and leave him alone and that he was sorry for what he'd done. When the screaming continued the guard went to the cell to tell Mr. Murphy to quiet down because he was disturbing others. He reported that when he arrived there was no one in the cell but Murphy who was, by this time, on the floor. So, Ms. Harrison, because Mr. Murphy is dead, the case is closed."

Sarah was stunned. Murphy was dead? How on earth could that be? Dead. "Well, thank you for your time and efforts Detective Carruthers," Sarah said shakily.

"Ms. Harrison even though there isn't anyone to change for the assault against you, the department's victims services counselor is available to you should you want someone to talk to about all of this."

Haunted Heart / Laverne Stewart

Sarah shook his hand and said she would call the number on the card he'd handed to her if she felt she was having trouble dealing with things. The vibration deep in the centre of her body seemed to be welling up, she wasn't sure how much longer she could keep herself in check.

Patrick then offered to walk the officer to the door and apologized for his temper. The detective told him to forget about it and then the two men walked out of the parlor and down the hall to the foyer where they shook hands and the officer left the house.

Sarah was still letting the aftershocks about the news of Murphy's death resound throughout her very core. She wasn't sure she understood what had happened before his heart attack, that part of what Carruthers had said left her feeling cold and a sense of expectation she truly could not understand. She still couldn't comprehend how someone as young and fit as him could have died this way.

Hannah, who'd been very quiet through the meeting, decided Sarah needed to hear fully what she knew the jail guard and the police department didn't, or at least didn't want to admit. Damned they were cowards, she thought. Patrick had returned to the parlor and sat down on the armchair by the fireplace once more.

"Don't be settin' yourself too easy there. I need to explain something about young Murphy's death to both of you. I knows ya both have heard the expression 'scared half to death?' Well it seems that no good redneck was scared all the way."

Patrick and Sarah stared at Hannah. "You mean." Patrick said, "that he was literally scared to death? Frightened so badly that he suffered a fatal heart attack? Hannah, please, this is not the time."

Hannah nodded her head. "Oh it can happen, indeed it can." Sarah felt her legs begin to give way and allowed her body to drop onto the settee.

"Don't you be looking at me like the old gal's lost the last brick in her dray neither," Hannah contined. "You of all people, Patrick, should not be so dense. You've read about the hounds how many times?"

Sarah just stared at the two of them, her confusion and exhaustion slowly being replaced by a knowing uncertainty.

"Hannah, I love Doyle's work, but really. Sir Charles Baskerville dies of a fatal heart attack, apparently because he is frightened to death by the hound. You can't think there were hounds in the cell."

Hannah reached over to Sarah, the trembling of Sarah's hands barely noticeable, but to Hannah they were like solid tremors. "Don't be so sure that what you cannot see, or refuse to see, is not there."

Patrick was musing that since Arthur Conan Doyle was a physician as well as an author, perhaps his story was based on medical knowledge, intuition, or literary license.

"I was curious whether fatal heart attacks and stress could cause someone's death or whether it's simply an interesting fictional story. You do know researchers at the University of California wondered about it too. Back in 2001 they conducted a study to see if there was a link between extreme stress and death." The nervousness of his timbre betrayed the calm Patrick was trying to portray with his ramblings. And Sarah knew it.

"Studies, researchers, all the same," Hannah sniffed, "this is about truth plain and simple."

Haunted Heart / Laverne Stewart

"If Murphy had a chronic heart condition a stress-induced heart attack could certainly kill him," Patrick thought aloud. We know his grandfather died of a heart attack 30 years ago. Maybe the Murphys all had weak, evil hearts."

"Evil heart or no, Evelyn Elizabeth Harrison paid Murphy a visit last night. She wanted him to understand that because of what he did, not only would he face a judge and jury here, he would also be judged by God almighty for the evil thing he did to our Sarah here," Hannah explained. Her eyes shone with the certainty of what she was saying. "I know Evelyn Elizabeth Harrison. She is a kind and gentle spirit but canno' stand anyone abusing a young lass, and she is very protective of our Sarah here."

Hannah slipped over closer on the settee and leaned her arm around Sarah's shoulders. "She has watched over you since the day you drew your first breath child, she will do what she can to make sure you are safe and others understand that they will answer for any harm that comes to you."

Before she could stop herself, visions of an apparition floating in menace above Murphy flashed like images in a horror film in Sarah's head, scenes that she could only draw on from the few low budget thrillers she had ever seen.

"Not like that girlie, never think of it like that," Hannah said. "For someone to be faced with the amount of pain they have caused and knowing that their evil deeds, carried out or not, are known in the spirit realm, is enough to lay any guilty man down. She did not plan him harm, only to make him see that he was found out."

Sarah, who'd listened to Patrick and Hannah's conversation, couldn't stand it any longer. "Will you listen to the two of you? If I didn't know better I'd swear the two of you were drunk, crazy or both. You're both talking nonsense." Lifting herself out of the settee she was ready to bolt out of the room.

"I refuse to believe that man was scared to death by a ghost who is my supposed 'spirit protector.' I have better things to do than to sit here and listen to any more of this. If you two want to sit by the fire and tell ghost stories that's up to you. I'm leaving."

"Where are you going girlie?"

"I don't know. Anywhere but here – and stay out of my head Hannah."

Hannah looked at Patrick. "Don't worry boy-o, she'll come to understand and accept in her time. You did. And if I can turn a disbeliever like you around to my way of thinking, she'll come to see the truth too."

"*Stay out of her head*, oh my land child, I'm sure you are not going to be liking what you just put into words. Nonbeliever me arse."

15

Sarah was feeling frustrated by everything and everyone.

The sooner she could sell this place and all of the stuff in it, the better, she thought. While still sore, she hardly felt the aches in her body because she was so emotional over the news that her attacker was dead and that Hannah insisted he'd died of fright after a visit from her spirit guide; the woman who'd once lived here.

Tomorrow morning, she would call Tim Isaac Auctioneers and have them come to give her an appraisal on the things she intended to sell.

She went into the bedroom where Evelyn Elizabeth Harrison had died. She looked around for something or someone to appear. "Ok Evelyn. Hannah says you are here to watch over me. Well let me tell you something. I don't believe in ghosts but if you are real what do you want with me?"

Just then Marmalade ran into the bedroom and rubbed against Sarah's legs and started to meow very loudly. "What do you want fur ball?"

The cat continued to meow and walked over to the armoire where Sarah had found the keys that unlocked the wooden chest where the love poems had been kept. The cat stood up on its hind legs and pawed at the door.

"What's in there fur ball?" Sarah opened the door and looked inside. Nothing. It appeared to be empty.

"You're as crazy as the rest of them here, do you know that Marmalade?"

The cat leaped onto the shelf inside and started pawing at the back of the piece of furniture. At first Sarah couldn't see anything. But when she leaned in she could see there was something different about the shelf. She ran her fingers around the wood. There was a notch on either side of the bottom of the shelf.

She picked up Marmalade and placed her back on the floor.

Sarah then placed her fingers in the notches and lifted up on the wood. It came up easily. This was a false bottom. Underneath she found a leather bound book with the initials EEH on the cover. It was Evelyn Elizabeth Harrison's journal. Sarah flipped it open and started to read...

May 7, 1847

Dear Diary,

Mr. Gallagher the horse trainer has accepted an invitation to dine with us this evening. Father wants to discuss the possibility of investing in Canadian Horses. I have never seen this breed but father says they are very much like the Morgan; very muscular, compact and stout, with a naturally animated gait.

Father is thinking about investing in this breed as they are considered to have soundness, hardiness and endurance as well as being willing horses that people would naturally want for their farms and carriages, I should think. Mr. Gallagher is expected to arrive at 7 o'clock. I am beside myself with anticipation. He is so handsome. I shall have to pay particular attention tonight to my attire.

Haunted Heart / Laverne Stewart

May 8, 1847

Dear Diary

Last evening was so delightful. Mr. Gallagher was such an amiable supper guest. He told us of his family's estate in Ireland and described the horses his father had bred there before they came to Canada. Tragic is this poor man's lot. Imagine having both of your parents die during the ships crossing; so many died of ship's fever while making the voyage.

On a more pleasant note, Mr. Gallagher is not only very handsome but extremely intelligent. He knows so much about horses and how to develop a strong and sturdy blood line. Father is most impressed with his knowledge of the Canadian Horse. He explained that it descended from the French stock Louis XIV sent to Canada some 200 years ago. The reason these horses are so popular, Mr. Gallagher says, is because they are so hardy and tend to thrive despite low comfort, hard work, and bad roads which is perfect for a farmers' needs.

Father plans to breed them and sell them to the farmers in the county.

Mr. Gallagher said these horses have nicknames like the little iron horse and the horse of steel. I could hardly eat any of my supper tonight, I was so engrossed in everything he said. Also, it was very hard not to stare at him for he is indeed a handsome man. I hope father shall invite him to dine with us again and frequently. Then again he is always in the stables working with the horses so I shall have to visit my new filly very often.

Haunted Heart / Laverne Stewart

June 9, 1847

Dear Diary,

He has asked me to look for notes that he says he will tuck into the rock wall and he will place a lady slipper flower on the top of the wall. I found my first note today. It was a poem he wrote to me. It said:

"I am here and yet am unseen

I am not as once I've been

Now I strive to prove my worth

To live again in joy, in mirth

See the man I truly am

I will rise in wealth again."

Sarah now understood how they met and what happened to end their romance but what was missing were all of the details in the middle. What took place between April 3, 1847 when Padraig Gallagher first arrived on the estate and July 16, 1847 the day Evelyn Elizabeth died.

Their romance lasted just three and a half months, and then they were both dead; Evelyn Elizabeth from an overdose of laudanum and Padraig Gallagher the victim of an accident with a team of horses.

"Whatever happened to the two of you?" Sarah wondered aloud.

She knew many of the answers would be contained in the diary but she didn't want to stay in the bedroom where the dead girl had died.

Sarah decided to take the diary into the room she was staying in down the hall to continue her reading. Marmalade followed her and jumped on the bed and settled down for a nap. Sarah looked at the cat.

"You could at least ask if you can stay before you make yourself at home."

It struck Sarah then that this was the cat's home. It was the cat's and Hannah's and even more of a home to Patrick than to her. Sarah needed to get this place out of her life and get back to Boston but as she thought of leaving the dear old woman and Patrick and even the cat, she thought home really is where you are loved and welcomed by people who care for you.

She also thought of her friends and co-workers at the restaurant. Chaz Alvarez was one of her closest friends. She missed him and decided it was time to call and hear a familiar voice. She picked up the phone in her bedroom and dialed the number. It rang a couple of times and then she heard his voice. "Hell-loo!"

"Hi Chaz. It's Sarah."

"Sarah, darling! How are you? Why you've had me worried sick. Just sick I tell you. You left here two weeks ago and I haven't heard a peep, not a whisper from you in all this time; shame on you Sunshine. Are you okay? Things are absolutely crazy down here. You've missed three fabulous parties. I hosted all of them; of course. I have tragic news though honey. The guy I thought was Mr. Right turned out to be a definite Mr. Wrong. That's why I threw the parties. I had to cheer myself up of course. Now enough about me what's new with you?"

Sarah told him about the estate and about the plans she had to restore the place so she could put it on the market. She described the home's furnishings and all of the beautiful architecture.

Chaz was practically beside himself with delight. He had always been fond of the Victorian period and knowing his friend was living in such a place made him practically drool.

"Who's doing the interior decorating for you? Tell me you haven't hired anybody. Why I will simply be crushed if you have. I want to come to Saint John for a visit. I have two weeks vacation time coming up. I'd love to get my hands on that place. Please let me help! Besides you must be terribly lonely in that huge mansion all by yourself."

"Actually Chaz, I'm not lonely at all."

She then told him about Marmalade as she scratched the cat behind the ears.

"And I'd love for you to meet Hannah. She's worked here for 50 years but she has more spirit and energy than most people half her age. She is a wonderful cook and a dear, sweet woman who has a heart of gold and a tongue as sharp as one of her kitchen knives, but if you are in her good books she will love you to the very end."

"So it's you and a cat and an old lady? Sarah darling you need me more than you know. Where's the excitement in your life?"

Haunted Heart / Laverne Stewart

Sarah wasn't sure she wanted to tell Chaz about Patrick.

The truth was she wasn't exactly sure what the nature of their relationship was at the moment. Hadn't she and Patrick agreed that this was nothing more than a summer time romance that would end in the fall with the sale of Harrison House? For the first time since she'd arrived here, the thought of leaving him made her feel sad and lonely.

"Chaz promise me you won't lose your mind if I tell you something?"

"Ooo darling, do you have gossip? Share with Chazie, you know how much I love juicy juice."

"Chaz it's not gossip. It's about me. I've met someone here."

"Darling! How wonderful! I want all the details! Don't leave anything out."

Sarah told him that Patrick Gallagher was the contractor she'd hired to do most of the restoration work on the mansion.

"Get to the good part. What does he look like? Is he hot?"

"He's tall, muscular, tanned and has black hair and the bluest eyes you've ever seen."

"Oooo he sounds absolutely yummy. I might just have to come up there and see if I can steal him away from you."

Sarah laughed. "Chaz he might be the type of guy you're attracted to, but I can assure you he wouldn't be interested in you. He's very, and I mean *very* straight. I shouldn't have waited to phone. I miss you Chaz. When do you think you'll be here?"

"I can arrive any time you want me there sweetie. I just have to make sure I have someone to cover off my shifts at the restaurant. By the way, everyone said that if I heard from you I should be sure to say hi for them. When do you want me there?"

Sarah told him the reproduction wallpaper should be delivered to the house within the next few weeks.

"It will be great to have you stay here with me Chaz. I can't wait to see you. Yes I love you too honey. Bye for now."

Sarah hung up the phone. Patrick was standing at the bedroom door. She wasn't sure what he'd heard but from the expression on his face she was pretty sure he had the wrong impression.

16

"Patrick that was my friend Chaz Alvarez. He's coming here for a visit. He's offered to help with the painting and the wallpaper. Isn't that great?"

"Yeah that's fantastic. Sarah, I packed a suitcase and had planned to stay with you here and I will but as soon as your Boston boyfriend gets here I should clear out of here and give you two your privacy. Three's a crowd as they say."

Sarah started to laugh.

"What's so funny?"

"You're jealous!"

"I am not. I am a little pissed though that you didn't tell me about Chaz What's-His-Name. You should have told me you were involved with someone else and I would never have gotten involved with you. I don't mess around in other people's business. I am sure he wouldn't appreciate the competition."

Sarah was laughing hard enough now that her cheeks and stomach started to ache and tears started to trickle down her face.

"Stop laughing," Patrick snapped. "It's not funny. I don't find it funny and I am sure your boyfriend won't either if he finds out the two of us have been having really hot sex while you've been apart. That makes you a cheater and I'm not into that so…"

Before he could say another word Sarah got up from the bed and walked over to him and placed her fingers on his mouth to shut him up.

"Patrick, Chaz Alvarez is my best friend... and he's gay. He's *very, very gay*. Now if you are finished with your jealous fit you can shut up and kiss me."

Sarah stood on her tiptoes and placed her lips where her fingers had been. Her mouth was still swollen and sore so it was light and delicate. But her fingers found their way to his butt and the caress let him know she was definitely interested in him and not gay old what's-his-name in Boston. "Now was there something you wanted to tell me?"

"I'm sorry I jumped to conclusions and I guess I was a little jealous."

"Anything else?"

"You've been through a terrible trauma Sarah that no one should experience. I simply want to be with you and to make sure you are safe. You're the most beautiful woman I have ever known and when you are healed both physically and emotionally and want to be with me again, I cannot wait to make love to you again. Until then I plan to sleep in the next bedroom."

Sarah was touched by his thoughtfulness. Patrick Gallagher was a beautiful man both inside and out. He was strong, protective and very caring; he was everything she dreamed of in a man. The only problem was he lived in this city and her life was in Boston. As soon as the work here was done she would have to say goodbye to him, but until then she would love every minute she had with him. The thought of leaving him made her feel very badly. She pushed it from her mind and decided to think of something else.

"I found Evelyn Elizabeth's diary. It was hidden in a false bottom of a drawer in the armoire in her old bedroom. I read a bit from it and so far I found out how they first met. Your ancestor Padraig arrived on the estate in April 1847. It seems Cornelius Harrison had hired him to train a horse he'd bought for his daughter. Within the next month he was advising old Cornelius about buying and breeding Canadian horses to sell. Evelyn Elizabeth was very smitten with him."

Patrick leaned down and gave her a gentle kiss on the cheek and whispered in her ear. "Not as smitten as I am with you."

Just then a very loud growling noise could be heard in the room. "Patrick maybe Hannah is right. Maybe this place is haunted. That is the scariest sound I have ever heard." The growling sound happened again and Sarah laughed. "Wow your stomach is a hungry beast. We better feed it before it attacks."

"That's why I came upstairs – to tell you that Hannah says supper is ready."

When they arrived in the kitchen Hannah had her hands on her hips and looked at Patrick.

"Did you get lost in this big old house?" Hannah asked. "I sent you upstairs ten minutes ago. Come on the pair of you, sit down and eat before everything goes cold."

Sarah hadn't eaten anything today. Her conversation with Chaz and the one she'd had after with Patrick had really brightened her mood. Suddenly she was very hungry. "Everything looks delicious Hannah. I'm starving!"

Hannah was both pleased and relieved. She had been so worried about the girl after what she'd been through last night. A healthy appetite was a sign that she was going to be just fine. All she needed was continued love and support and the emotional scars would eventually heal as well as the cuts and bruises.

"I've decided the best thing for me to do to get over what happened to me, is to stay busy. I want to continue to work with you to catalogue the contents of the house and decide what's to be donated to the museum. I know the work crew will be here first thing in the morning and you will be busy with them, but when you have some free time perhaps you can help me. I plan to go through the rooms on the third floor tomorrow. I think I can fill out the forms on my own and then you can look over the paperwork when you have some free time."

Hannah clucked like an old mother hen. "You'll do nothing of the kind young woman. Why just look at you. You need to rest another couple of days before you'll be able to go back to work on this place. As soon as supper is over, you march yourself right back upstairs to bed. The most you should be doing is holding a book in your hands. You need to rest girlie. Do you hear me?"

"Yes Hannah."

Sarah smiled. This old woman was very devoted to those she loved. For the first time Sarah felt what she imagined it would feel like to have a mother or grandmother fussing over her. She felt warm and secure in this place with these two people. She would be sad to leave them. Perhaps she would even be sad to sell Harrison House.

"There now girlie you eat up and let old Hannah take care of you for a few days. I need someone to fuss over and you need to be coddled a wee bit. We'll worry about what's to come when the time comes. For now let's just let things be."

How did she do that, Sarah wondered. Hannah seemed to know just what to say and when to say it. She never voiced her thoughts aloud and yet Hannah seemed to know. Maybe she was sensitive or gifted after all.

Hannah patted her hand and gave her a wink. Patrick had been quiet throughout dinner. He was thinking of Sarah and what also was to come at the end of the summer. He was falling in love with this woman and the descent was fast and furious. He'd never felt so in love with any woman before and it would kill him to see her leave when the summer was over. How was he going to convince her not to sell Harrison House and to stay here with him?

"Yes t'is good to let things happen as they will," Hannah said as she looked at Patrick. All is well tonight and the future will take care of itself. Now, I have a lovely dish of fresh strawberries and cream for anyone who wants it. Can I pour anyone a second cup of tea?"

Hannah had a meeting at the church and left as soon as the kitchen had been tidied from supper.

Sarah was still feeling tired and sore and decided she'd go back to bed to rest and read more from Evelyn Elizabeth's diary.

Patrick wasn't sure what to do with the rest of the evening. He needed to go back to his house to catch up on paperwork but he didn't want to leave Sarah alone.

Haunted Heart / Laverne Stewart

"Patrick, I'm fine. I want to rest. The doors will be locked and I will be completely fine here on my own. You go do what you have to do. I want to read more from the diary anyway."

Patrick reluctantly agreed to leave her but only as long as she called him to assure him everything was fine here while he was gone.

He assured her he would be back in a few hours and he tucked her back into bed before he placed a gentle kiss on her forehead and left.

Sarah wasn't used to being fussed over. It was strange but at the same time made her feel warm inside. She picked up the diary and continued where she left off.

May 12, 1847

Dear Diary

While I was in the stable today Mr. Gallagher handed me a lady slipper flower and said that it reminded him of me. When I asked him why, he said its meaning was 'capricious beauty'. Then he laughed and said indeed he found me unpredictable and impulsive. I told him I was no such thing and I pretended to be insulted but I believe he could see through to the truth. Indeed I completely gave myself away when I blushed and smiled as he told me he thought the lady slipper is one of the most beautiful flowers but it in no way can compete with my own beauty.

He touched my hand and asked for permission to call me Evelyn and he insisted I call him Padraig. I consented of course and then he kissed me. It was the first time I have ever been kissed. I have often wondered what it would be like to feel such intimacy. It far exceeded my expectations. I could feel shivers go through my entire body.

We agreed that since he was employed by my father it would be best to keep our feelings for one another private until such time as Padraig had an opportunity to speak to my father and ask permission to court me. Until then we shall meet secretly. He will place a lady slipper on the rock wall nearest to the stables any time he is free to meet as he will know when the stables will be vacant so we can see one another.

May 13, 1847

Dear Diary

I found a lady slipper on the garden wall and beneath it was a note. It said 'My lady I can think of nothing but that kiss and your lovely face. You have me completely besotted and hardly able to concentrate today. If you are able, please meet me this afternoon at the stables.'

This afternoon mother has sewing circle and father will be attending to his business at the port as one of his ships is nearly ready to be launched. I will tell mother I cannot go with her to sewing circle because I have a headache. This will provide a couple of hours to be with Padraig. I know I am dishonoring mother and father by telling this lie. I hope they and God will forgive me but I must be true to my heart and my heart tells me it is right to go to Padraig this afternoon.

At 2 p.m. I went to the stables. I could hardly breathe I was so nervous and so excited. Padraig was waiting for me there. Father and mother had taken one of the carriages when they left after dinner.

Haunted Heart / Laverne Stewart

The second one was rigged with my little filly. Padraig said he asked father's permission to take it out for a ride to give her a good run and to see how she is coming along in her training. He didn't tell father that I would be coming along for the ride as well. He sat up front while I sat alone inside. I wondered where he was taking me. We rode for about 20 minutes and then the carriage stopped. Padraig opened the carriage door and helped me down from it. We were in a most beautiful wooded area. I immediately recognized it as Lilly Lake. I had heard it was a favourite spot for young lovers but I had never been here before. If I die tomorrow I shall go to my reward the happiest woman on the earth. It was the most wonderful afternoon of my life.

Padraig handed me a bouquet of wild flowers. He placed a blanket on the ground and we sat and enjoyed the view of ducks swimming in the water. We talked about his childhood and I told him about my life. All too soon it was time to return home. He helped me up into the carriage. Instead of closing the door and taking the reigns he climbed inside with me and closed the door.

We sat there looking at one another. I was unsure of what to do. I felt my face redden and I turned away. Slowly he turned me back toward him and he leaned closer. I knew he was going to kiss me. God help me I know it's a sin to be so intimate with this man that I am not engaged to, but I couldn't stop the passion that I felt at that moment. I have never felt such desire. I hardly knew that kind of passion existed. Then I felt his fingers on my bodice. He looked into my eyes unsure of whether to advance further. Just as he was about to remove his hands I told him I wanted him. He makes me feel bold and my desire for him is beyond all reason. I begged him to take me. In that moment I couldn't see past the need to feel his hands and mouth on me. I closed my eyes waiting for what was to come next and then it all stopped.

He told me: "No Evelyn. Not like this. I want you desperately but I want it to be perfect and a carriage is no place. I want our first time together to be one we will not regret but will look back on with fondness in our old age. I shall not approach you in this way again until your father has given me permission to court you and I have his consent to allow us to marry. Evelyn Elizabeth Harrison would you make me the happiest man in the world and be my wife?"

I could hardly speak. The words would not come so I nodded as tears of joy filled my eyes. We kissed and then he told me he would take me home and would approach my father at the earliest opportunity. Oh how I wish and pray the answer will be yes.

May 14, 1847

Dear Diary,

The minutes are passing as hours today. I had to endure one of mother's sewing circles at our home today. The ladies in attendance talked on and on about the usual church gossip. I kept looking out the window for any sign of Patrick. I hoped I would see him in the field working one of the horses.

One of the ladies noticed me staring out the window and when she caught sight of Padraig she inquired who it was I was looking at. Mother answered for me. She said he was the hired groom and horse trainer who'd been in the family's employment for nearly six weeks. Mrs. Harold Spencer said he was indeed handsome but no lady should ever stare at a man; especially the hired help.

Haunted Heart / Laverne Stewart

Mother agreed and told me to turn my attention back to my embroidery. How can they only see the servant? It shall, I fear, not bode well for Padraig and I when he asks for permission to marry if this is how mother feels. I hope father can be convinced otherwise...

Sarah read until her eye's were getting heavy. She looked at the clock. It was 10:30. Just then the phone beside her bed rang. It was Patrick.

"You haven't called. Are you okay?"

Sarah smiled. "Yes. I am fine. I have been spending the past couple of hours reading about our ancestors. It seems they were carrying on a secret love affair. He wanted to marry her and was about to ask her father's permission. She was absolutely head over heels for him and from what she has written about his behaviour toward her, I do believe he felt the same. How could things have gone so horribly wrong?"

"Maybe something she has written further in her diary will give you the answer," Patrick mused. "I just wanted to let you know I am on my way back. I should be there in another 15 minutes or so."

"Okay that's fine. See you then."

Sarah hung up the phone and then closed the diary and put it on her nightstand. The phone rang several times – no one was on the line each time she answered.

The phone rang again. She picked it up.

"Hello? Hello? Who's there? Look this isn't funny. If this is some kind of a practical joke I can find out who made this call by dialing star-69."

There was silence on the line and then she heard the dial tone again. "Creep!" Sarah said as she hung up the phone.

The phone rang again. She picked it up and didn't wait. "Look whoever you are I don't have time for this. So do me a favour and drop dead."

"Sarah? What in the name of God is wrong with you girlie? It's Hannah. I wanted to let you know I was back from the church and I was calling to see how you are and ask if you needed anything before I went to bed."

"Oh Hannah. I'm sorry. Someone just called here and didn't say anything before they hung up the phone. It was probably just some kid playing practical joke."

"Oh darlin' did it frighten you? I'm sure it did. Do you want me to sleep in the main house tonight?"

"No I'm fine. Besides Patrick is on his way over. He will be in the bedroom right next door should I need anything. You go to bed. I'll see you in the morning."

"All right then. I'll say good night to you then. Sleep well now."

"You too Hannah; goodnight."

Sarah hung up the phone.

In the living room of the apartment above the garage Hannah sat sipping tea talking to an old, unseen friend.

"You are determined to do whatever it takes to bring these two together. Keeping her a little nervous to make her need Patrick even more. I know it was you that made that telephone ring. You always were a very determined girl Evelyn Elizabeth."

Haunted Heart / Laverne Stewart

17

Sarah fell asleep while waiting for Patrick to return.

When Patrick came into her bedroom he found the light on. He pulled the blankets up around her shoulders and shut out the light.

She truly was a beautiful woman and the one Patrick knew he wanted to spent the rest of his life with. But he didn't see much hope of a future for them. Hadn't she said all she wanted was some fun and that it would all be over when the job here was done?

Hannah said all would be well, and Patrick hoped she was right. It was getting late and he knew the crew would be back on site at 8 a.m. so he needed to go to bed too. He went into the room next door and slipped out of his shirt and jeans and crawled beneath the sheets.

Sarah awoke in the middle of the night. She wasn't sure what woke her and since she wasn't tired she decided to read more from the diary...

May 15, 1847

Dear Diary,

I found another lady slipper this morning on the garden wall. There was a note tucked into a rock crevice beneath it that said 'Meet me if you can this afternoon. I have a great need to see your beautiful face and to hear your sweet voice; until then and God willing my darling I will.' The minutes are passing as hours today. I shall have to endure more of mother's sewing circle after lunch. This time the conversation will surely be about the plans mother is making for a ball in my honour. It will be my introduction to society. I know I should be excited about this, but presently, and since his arrival at Harrison House, I have but one thought, one desire and that is to be with my dearest Padraig. It is my fondest wish that since he and father are working to secure, breed and sell the Canadian horses I might be able to convince father to invite him to the ball. How wonderful it would be to waltz with him. How I would be the envy of all of the girls there to be in the arms of such a handsome man. I will die if I cannot see him this afternoon. Perhaps I might convince mother to allow me to return home early from the sewing circle. Father shan't be home from the shipyards until after six o'clock. The sewing circle usually doesn't conclude until 4:30. So if I leave at 2:30 that would leave us a couple of hours to visit with one another. Please God I ask this with all my heart.

May 16, 1847

Dear Diary

I am in love. It is so deep I hardly thought it possible to feel so much that I can hardly contain myself. Mother agreed to allow me to return home on my own. I told her I was concerned about the health of Daisy, my filly, as she seemed to be off her feed this morning. Yes it's a fib and I know I should not tell these untruths but I needed to get to the stables and I could think of nothing else to say.

I arrived there at 2:30. When I arrived he was there polishing leather saddles. He looked up and smiled in such a way that I was sure I should faint right there on the spot.

Haunted Heart / Laverne Stewart

Since our time was very limited and we wanted to be alone, I suggested that he help me up into the hay loft. It was warm there. A little too warm but I didn't care.

Padraig surprised me with a tiny bouquet of wild flowers. He kissed me then and if I should die tonight I would have no regrets for that moment was perfect. Then he said: "I have some very good news. Your father has invited me to come to the ball your parents are hosting in your honour. I do hope you shall save room on your dance card for me."

How wonderful! He is to come to the dance. Thank you God!

Then he told me how much he loved me and vowed that as soon as the opportunity presented itself following the ball, he would ask my father's permission for us to court and soon thereafter to wed and then he kissed me and said 'I love you Evelyn Elizabeth Harrison. I think I loved you from the moment I saw you. Do you love me Evelyn? Do you really want to be my wife? You know all of my family's fortune is gone but as I stand here today I make this vow. I will get it all back and I will keep you in the fashion to which a lady should be kept. We shall have a wonderful life together and will be happy for as long as we both shall live.' I was overcome in that moment and I asked him to kiss me once more.

I looked into his eyes. They were so intensely blue. I inhaled deeply has he bent his head down and kissed my neck. He stood behind me and as he continued to kiss me, his fingers unfastened the buttons at the back of my favourite pale pink dress. He stopped himself and said it couldn't be like this and that he wanted our first time to be special and in a fine feather bed. I begged him not to stop and said I had a great need for him in that moment. It didn't matter to me whether the mattress was hay or feather for in that moment all I could think of was how he was making my body feel. He whispered his desire for me and then he continued in his efforts to free me from the silk and ruffles of my dress. The only pleasing thing about it in this moment was that it gave him a good view of my breasts and its capped sleeves allowed him to touch the skin on my arms which sent shivers down my back. He told me that he wished fashion for ladies didn't dictate that they wear several layers of undergarments. Once the dress had fallen to the floor he concentrated next on removing my chemise. Next, he freed me from my petticoat. When it was out of the way he concentrated on my corset. When it was free so were my breasts. This was the first time any man had seen them and yet I felt no shame. He told me they were beautiful and he asked permission to touch them. He did so first with his hands and then with his mouth. He lowered me to the hay and then, when I thought I could stand no more, he stripped himself of his clothing and then lay beside me. We lay facing one another. He told me that it was important that he do this right for he knew this was my first time. He kissed me slowly and deeply. His tongue licked my lips and coaxed them to part. His tongue explored my mouth. I moaned and moaned and moved my hips. His hand traced lazy circles on my stomach as he moved closer to my thighs. He slipped a hand between my legs and gently pushed them apart. With his fingers he gently massaged me down there. He told me that I was very wet and he asked if I would allow his mouth to explore where his fingers had been. I nodded but was too overcome to speak. His tongue darted in and out of me. Then he settled his mouth on me and sucked until I felt myself explode inside. I was the most glorious feeling.

Next he positioned himself above me and parted my legs with his hands. Gently he entered me and pushed. He told me it would only hurt for a moment and then the pain would give way to pleasure. I tried not to cry and then, the pain was gone and was soon replaced with wave upon wave of delight. Together we moved as one until he could no longer hold back. He filled me fully with his seed and we lay together in one another's arms, both satisfied with our union. He looked ashamed of himself and said that he'd been overcome with desire and that he wished that what we had done would have waited for our wedding night. But I assured him that I did not regret our union and that I felt as though we already were as one and that surely God wouldn't punish us for our love, for a love as strong as ours couldn't be denied or restrained. He then laughed and said that my candor was one of the things he loved most about me. At this point it was after four o'clock and I knew that I must return to the house in case mother arrived home early from the church. Padraig told me to be sure to wash thoroughly and to make sure I washed my undergarments so the maid wouldn't have any evidence of what we had done to bring to my mother's attention. We kissed and pledged our love to one another again both vowing to find a way to be together again as soon as possible.

June 17, 1847

Dear Diary,

I found another lady slipper flower on the rock wall with something sweet tucked inside. It was another poem and it said:

"Maiden, maiden fair of face

Eyes of green in state of grace

Voice as soft as feather down

Beauty in the pale pink gown

Haunted Heart / Laverne Stewart

See me here, watch me now

You have me on my knees and how."

As Sarah continued to read these diary entries she could feel her desire for Patrick growing. It was very early in the morning. She left her bed and went into the room where he slept. She slipped out of her cotton night gown. She slid into the bed beside him.

"Sarah what are you…?"

"Shhhh…Patrick. I've been doing some research on our ancestors. Seems my Evelyn and I have something in common. We both have had the pleasure of being with incredibly sexy, hot Gallagher men who know how to touch a woman in all the right places. I have a great need for you to touch me again."

"Are you sure? You're pretty banged up."

"So you will be slow and gentle. I want you Patrick. Now."

Neither said another word as Patrick kissed her for the next hour and they explored one another's bodies until they were both aching with a desire so great neither could contain it any longer. He stroked her womanhood until she screamed his name aloud and begged him to take her.

"Please Patrick I need to feel you inside me. I need you to fill me up. Please Patrick now. Give it to me."

"I will – but not just yet." With that said, Patrick moved down between her legs and lowered his mouth on to her.

His tongue tasted her juices; slowly at first and then faster and faster until he felt her release. Only then did he enter her. Together they moved in a slow, sensual dance. Back and forth, higher and higher they climbed until this time it was Patrick who was overcome with emotion and desire for her.

"Sarah, oh Sarah. I can't hold on much longer. You feel so good."

And in that moment they were overcome with a tidal wave so powerful that after they came to orgasm they were unable to speak.

Sarah was on her side. For the first time since they started making love she noticed the portrait of Cornelius and Mrs. Harrison hanging above them. Their stern faces almost seemed to be staring down disapprovingly at their act of carnal pleasure.

Sarah refused to look at the painting any more but decided that she didn't like it or any of the other portraits in the house – except for the one of Evelyn Elizabeth – and she would give all of them to the museum if it wanted them.

They fell asleep in one another's arms and hardly moved until the sun broke through the window just after 7 a.m.

Patrick got up and showered and dressed.

Sarah remained asleep for another hour and only woke when the sound of the work crew grew loud enough that it roused her.

She got up and showered and then dressed quickly. She was surprised at how much better she felt. Hardly any body aches. The swelling around her mouth from where Murphy had hit her was nearly gone thanks to Hannah's essential oils.

Sarah heard her stomach growling and couldn't wait to see if Hannah had made something wonderful for breakfast.

As she walked down the hall the aroma of waffles, bacon and coffee filled the air. "Good morning Hannah how are you today?"

"Well, well you sure did get up on the right side of the bed this morning didn't you girlie. You are looking much better than you did yesterday. But you be sure to take it easy. It's not good to push yourself."

"Hannah I'm absolutely fine. I'm not sore and I want to get back to work here. I thought while Patrick is busy with the work crew, I'd get to work sorting through the things I want to donate to the museum on the third floor. There is so much here. It's going to take at least several weeks to go through everything," Sarah said.

"Oh, and Hannah," she added. "I want you to have anything you want in the house. You've got a lifetime invested in this place. There must be some things here you'd like to have."

"No girlie. I have all that I want and need in my apartment. I never was one for things. I am sure you will do the right thing with the house and it's contents when the time comes."

Sarah knew the right thing in Hannah's mind was to keep it in the Harrison name and not to sell it and its contents to some stranger, but to Hannah's credit she didn't try to make her feel guilty about her plans to sell.

So, if no one was trying to make her feel badly, then why was she? For the first time since she arrived here over two weeks ago, Sarah was overcome with the feeling that she was betraying her family and that she was making a mistake in preparing this place for a new owner.

She took a sip from a cup of coffee that Hannah had handed her and she tried to push the thought from her head. It refused to leave. It remained with her all through breakfast too. When she excused herself and went to the third floor, the nagging feeling that she was doing the wrong thing kept at her.

Hannah washed up the breakfast dishes and smiled a little smile.

"It's working Evelyn. She's coming around to our way of thinking. Give her some more time and that girlie will do the right thing. I promise you that."

For the next three weeks the work on the house continued. Everything that had to be done on the exterior was complete and Sarah was very pleased with the work. The exterior of the building had been restored to its former glory and the grounds were lovelier than any park she'd seen.

She and Patrick worked tirelessly cataloging everything in the home that she planned to donate or to put up for auction.

Although they were very tired each night, they still had the energy and the desire to make love, which they did, and they enjoyed one another fully.

Sarah also found time to read passages in Evelyn's diary. The entries she read continued until the night Padraig Gallagher died. They told her much of their passion for one another.

Haunted Heart / Laverne Stewart

May 22, 1847

Dear Diary,

For the past week mother has been busy with her volunteer work at the hospital every afternoon and father is at the shipyard overseeing the latest construction.

I have been making my way to the stables to visit with Padraig. Some days we are with one another in the hay loft. Other times he takes me to our secluded spot at Lilly Lake and always it is glorious to be in his arms.

Padraig sometimes expresses his concern over whether father will deem him worthy enough to consent to our marriage. I have told him that I will marry him no matter what my father thinks. To be disowned by my family would not be half as devastating to me as losing the man whom I know God has meant to be my husband.

I have told Padraig that anything is possible if you want it badly enough.

Padraig has said some day he will own an estate like the one his family left behind in Ireland and that its stables will be filled with fine horses and our home shall be filled with many children and that all of them will have hair as red as mine.

I told him that none of our children will have red hair. They shall all have their father's good looks, dark hair and eyes as blue as the Atlantic Ocean.

Haunted Heart / Laverne Stewart

June 15, 1847

Dear Diary,

Mother has been very preoccupied with the ball she and father are hosting in my honour. There is so much to do. Indeed it will be wonderful and all because this is the night that Padraig plans to ask my father for my hand.

I have decided to wear my white gown with the emerald green satin sash. It has matching gloves and a bonnet and it is the prettiest gown I think I have ever seen. I hope Padraig likes it.

The invitations have all been sent and replies are coming back. It will be a wonderful occasion. I hope the weather is fine but one can never be certain. In July this city can be shrouded in fog and it can be rather cool while just outside the city it's hot and sunny. We shall have to hope for pleasant weather on July 6th.

June 18, 1847

Dear Diary,

I found another note in the rock wall with the lady slipper on top. Of course it was from my Padraig. He said in three weeks time, God willing, we would be engaged. He's written me more poetry. I have placed all of them in a keepsake box and have hidden it in the floor of my bedroom closest. Here is the latest one:

"*Lady fair from afar*

I am here and there you are

My fondest wish; to kiss your face

Haunted Heart / Laverne Stewart

To hold you in a warm embrace

Some day soon Lord I pray

We shall see our wedding day"

June 25, 1847

Dear Diary

Mother and Father have been very busy over the past week. He at the shipyard and she with the arrangements for the ball and her volunteering at the hospital so there has been little need to make excuses for my time and accounting for what I have been doing. Almost every afternoon we manage to be together, Padraig and I. It's wonderful to be with him.

We are making plans for our wedding. I hope to convince mother of a small yet beautiful affair in the garden this September. It is my favourite month and in this city it is the most beautiful. A garden wedding; how wonderful!

June 28, 1847

Dear Diary,

Today I am feeling unwell. Perhaps it is something I've eaten or maybe it is an illness I have come into contact with. Mother and father have insisted that I rest so that I may be well enough to attend the ball next Saturday.

I have never had an illness such as this. I am very ill in the morning and then my stomach seems to settle itself and I am fine for the rest of the day. But then the next morning I am sick all over again and I am so very tired.

Haunted Heart / Laverne Stewart

I am so desperate to see Padraig but mother insists that I remain in bed. As soon as I am able I will get dressed and go to see him.

Sarah stopped reading for a moment and mused: *"She was pregnant?! Oh no. So romantic and so tragic. But what happened?"* Sarah then resumed reading, to learn more:

July 6, 1847

Dear Diary

I am still unwell but I have managed to convince mother and father that I am perfectly fine. I have told Padraig of my symptoms and he has explained to me that we are going to have a baby. He told me he was thrilled and although my parents would be furious with us at first, they would have to agree to a wedding as soon as possible.

Tonight we shall tell them and tonight we shall be man and wife, he says. It might not be the garden wedding of my dreams but I shall marry the man of my dreams and that is all that matters.

He wrote this to me today: My dearest bride-to-be. I am counting the hours until I am able to ask permission to marry you. I know they shall be angry with us for what we have done, but I trust that when they realize we are going to have their grandchild, they will understand that this marriage is meant to be. I can hardly wait to say my wedding vows to you before God and your parents. Ours will be a blessed union and our baby will know the love between his parents was ordained by God. All of my love, Padraig.

Haunted Heart / Laverne Stewart

And he wrote me this poem:

"Lady fair now not so far

Thanks to God here we are

My heart's desire is coming true.

My only wish: to be with you

Our lives entwined will start tonight

Meet me under pale moonlight."

Sarah went to the online archives and found the death notices from the July 7, 1847 edition of the newspaper. Padraig Ryan Gallagher's name was there. It said the 18-year-old died suddenly after being trampled by a team of horses.

How could Padraig, a man who knew so much about horses, have been killed in this way and on that night? Then Evelyn Elizabeth was dead just three days later after a laudanum overdose. What happened? There were no other journal entries after July 6th. Sarah hoped she would find out somehow.

It was really time to get back to work. The rooms on the third floor had been cleared of furniture and now it was time to begin the painting and wallpapering here.

Chaz was due to arrive today and promised to stay for a couple of weeks to help as much as he could with the work.

The house should be ready for a real estate sign within the next month and she would be headed back to Boston. So why wasn't she excited?

18

Chaz Alvarez arrived, as usual, in a flourish. He gave Sarah a huge hug after she opened the door and invited him inside.

"Darling, I'm here! What a terribly long drive. I am simply exhausted. But I am not too tired to see this gorgeous place. The outside is simply spectacular. But oh dear, we *do* need some work in here don't we. Who in hell committed the crimes against décor by putting up that horrible wallpaper? It simply must go – but oooh, just look at the architecture and the furniture. Sarah darling, look at this furniture! I would simply kill or die to have some of it!"

Sarah took him through the entire mansion and then suggested they have some tea before she showed Chaz to his room. She took him to the kitchen where they found Hannah baking.

"Well who have we here?" Chaz asked.

Sarah introduced her friend to Hannah. The old lady decided she liked him when he praised Harrison House and told Hannah he thought Sarah was making a huge mistake selling such a treasure and perhaps between the two of them they could convince her to change her mind.

Hannah invited him and Sarah to have some of the tea biscuits she'd just made with a cup of Earl Grey. When he gushed about how good the biscuits were he was in Hannah's good books for sure.

"Sarah, I have prepared Evelyn's room for Chaz." Hannah smiled. "I'm sure he'd like to freshen up after that long drive. Chaz, you will find the room has a private bathroom. There are fresh towels laid out for you but if you need anything else just let me know. Supper will be at six."

Over tea, the three talked about the painting and wallpapering that needed to be done in every room to replace that which had been installed in the early 1980s.

"Those colours of teal and dusty rose are simply all wrong for the Victorian period" Chaz said. "Sarah has a really good eye for period appropriate colors and patterns. She showed me some of the reproduction wallpaper and it is perfect. In no time this place will be back to its original splendor. Sarah darling I really do need to shower and change out of these clothes. Do you mind showing me to my room please?"

Sarah and Chaz said so long to Hannah and walked down the hallway and up the two flights of stairs.

"Who is Evelyn?"

Sarah knew how easily frightened Chaz could get and how vivid his imagination could be at times so she decided not to tell him that her ancestor had died in the room where he was staying. "Oh she was one of my ancestors. It's a lovely room. I am sure you will love staying in here."

Sarah laughed at the amount of luggage he brought for his two-week stay.

"Well you just never know where you will be and what you'll be doing," Chaz explained, "so I like to pack for any and all occasions, Sarah."

"Well there is plenty of room to put your things in the closet, armoire and chest of drawers so I will leave you to unpack and freshen up," Sarah replied. "When you feel like it, join me in the bedroom down the hall and to the left. I'm there stripping wallpaper. Patrick Gallagher is the project manager here and you'll get to meet him as soon as he returns from the New Brunswick Museum where he went to deliver a truck load of things I'm donating from Harrison House."

By the time Chaz had showered, changed clothes and was helping strip wallpaper in one of the bedrooms, Patrick had returned and Sarah introduced them. She could tell that the two of them were assessing one another but keeping their opinions to themselves.

The three of them worked on removing all of the wallpaper in the room when Hannah came upstairs to tell them supper was on the table. The meal was, as usual, perfect and delicious. Chaz, who normally ate like a bird, said he would have to be careful or he would get a pot belly while he was here. He was openly flirting with Patrick who tried to ignore the advances. So did Hannah but Sarah was having a very hard time not laughing out loud at the winks and smiles Chaz was sending to Patrick. She knew he was deliberately testing Patrick to see whether he was homophobic. To Patrick's credit, if he was uncomfortable, he didn't appear to be.

Patrick told them that the painting crew would be here in the morning. They agreed that Sarah and Chaz would continue to strip the wallpaper and as soon as the rooms where ready, the painters would come in and do their work.

After supper Chaz decided to stroll the grounds and asked who wanted to join him. Hannah was going out to her card club and Patrick said he needed to take care of paperwork so it was just Sarah who agreed to walk with him.

Haunted Heart / Laverne Stewart

"Darling that man is absolutely delicious and from the way he was looking at you, I could tell he thinks you are pretty sweet too. Tell me, have the two of you been taking some time out from all of the work to have some fun together? Those four-poster feather beds would be fun to play on with someone as fine as Patrick."

Sarah didn't say a word but the blush that swept over her face told him everything he needed to know. "Seems like my Sarah has been a naughty girl! Good for you darling. That dry spell was lasting way too long. I am happy for you darling."

As they walked the expansive property, Chaz marveled at the landscaping and how beautifully everything had been done. The old water features had been restored and were now in operation. "This place would make a fabulous inn. Everything is perfect for just such a thing. Each bedroom has its own private bath and these Victorians are very popular with tourists. Why don't you stay here and start one? I need a place to escape to and I think this one would do very nicely darling."

Sarah made a face and then laughed. "Chaz you come up with the craziest ideas. I have no idea how to run an inn and besides my life is back in Boston."

Chaz stopped walking and suddenly he became serious which was very unlike him. "Darling I love you so I don't want you to take what I am about to say the wrong way. I want you to listen very carefully to me and think about what I am going to say to you before you make any decisions about getting rid of this place. Sarah, you work as a server at a Boston restaurant. You take night courses at a university. You have no family left there. And although I know I am fabulous, even I am not reason enough for you to stay in Boston. Look at this place Sarah. Most people can only dream of owning an estate like this. Thanks to this and your inheritance you don't have to work. There is an old lady in there that loves you like a daughter; who wants to take care of you and only an idiot wouldn't want to be with that gorgeous man. Why would you give all of this up to return to a restaurant job, some design courses and a boring old apartment? Like I said, I need a place to come for vacations and I bet you wouldn't have to try too hard to convince your other friends to come here to visit you. I am serious Sarah, you will be making a huge mistake if you sell this place and leave these people. Think about what you are doing will you please? If I owned this place, no one would be able to make me leave it. As a matter of fact, I might become a permanent house guest. Sarah I love you darling but your life is meant to be lived to the fullest and I think it's going to happen here with that man in this place, not alone in a Boston apartment. Now I have said all I am going to say and I won't pester you about it any more."

Sarah knew better than to argue with Chaz and promised to think about what he'd said, but she still didn't see how it would be possible to make a life here. Didn't Patrick say it was a summer time thing? How much did she really know him? He could have several women in his life. No, this was a business relationship with fringe benefits and when the job was done, he would go on with his life here and she would return to her old life in Boston. There was no sense getting attached to him or Hannah or Harrison House. Try as she might to convince herself of this, she knew it was too late. In five weeks she had fallen under the spell of this estate and knew leaving it and Hannah and Patrick would be incredibly hard – but it was something she'd have to do.

The painting crew arrived early the next morning and made quick work of the woodwork in the rooms on the third floor. The crisp white paint really brightened up the place. When the woodwork was dry the wallpaper was put up. The ornate patterns would have proven difficult to match for less experienced workers but the wallpaper installers on Patrick's crew were very good and had no trouble getting the job done. By the end of the week the bedrooms had been transformed. Chaz and Sarah decided that in order to appeal to viewers, all of the rooms in the mansion needed to be staged and so they spent their time arranging furniture to show each room to its fullest potential.

The two weeks Chaz had been here went by very quickly. The night before he was to leave they sat in the parlor chatting. Hannah was keeping everyone amused with Irish folklore. Some of the stories she told were funny and others were of ghosts and banshees.

"The story of the banshee began as a fairy woman who mourned the death of people she loved. In later stories, the appearance of the banshee could foretell death. Banshees, it's said, appear for certain Irish families. The banshee can appear in a variety of guises. Most often she appears as an ugly, frightening hag, but she can also appear as a stunningly beautiful woman. In the southwest of Ireland, her keen is experienced as a low, pleasant singing but in the north, it is heard as the sound of two boards being struck together and on Rathlin Island it's a thin, screeching sound somewhere between a crying woman and a hooting owl. Now, it's getting late and I have put in a long day as have you all. I'm going to bed. I'll say good night to you now. Pleasant dreams."

Patrick walked Hannah to her apartment above the garage while Sarah and Chaz stayed in the parlor. She could tell Hannah's ghost stories had spooked him. "Don't worry Chaz it's all a matter of the mind. If you think ghosts are real then they are. If you refuse to accept it as anything other than stories and nonsense, then you have nothing to worry about. Chaz was nervous but said he would try not to let Hannah's stories bother him.

Then, Patrick returned and Chaz said goodnight to them both and went up to Evelyn's room.

Patrick and Sarah went into her room and closed the door. They turned off the light and made love very quietly as they had ever since Chaz had arrived. As they lay in one another's arms, sleep came quickly because they were both very tired from all of the work they'd been doing in the house.

Just down the hall, Chaz had fallen asleep after he told himself several times Hannah's stories were the imagination of an old lady and the folklore of the Irish. Then he was startled when he heard someone crying.

"Sarah darling is that you? Chaz asked. "Sarah what's wrong?"

Chaz looked and saw her standing on the balcony. He got out of bed and put his silk bathrobe on. Then he walked to the balcony doors. He looked through the leaded glass and he could see her pacing back and forth. She was crying. "Sarah honey what's wrong?" he asked again.

He opened the balcony door and saw her standing there. But she was wearing a long white gown with a green satin sash, long white gloves and a green bonnet with a white bow. "Sarah?"

"Padraig! Padraig!"

Suddenly Chaz realized this wasn't Sarah. He blinked and the crying woman in the long white gown was gone. He screamed so loudly that Sarah and Patrick were woken. They quickly dressed and ran to the bedroom. Chaz was throwing clothing into suitcases and talking out loud to himself.

Haunted Heart / Laverne Stewart

"I have seen a lot of things and I can handle a lot. I don't even get too bent out of shape when people mix plaids and stripes or orange and pink but this place, this place is simply too much. I saw her! I saw that ancestor of yours. She was here calling for Patrick or Padraig or, oh I don't know what she said and I don't care! This place is haunted. I am not staying here another minute."

"Chaz what happened? Chaz calm down and tell us what happened," Sarah urged.

They all went into the kitchen where Sarah made him a cup of herbal chamomile tea. His hands were shaking and his skin was pale. Whatever he'd seen had really frightened him.

Chaz told them both that he woke up when he heard someone crying. He looked out of the windows in the balcony door and saw what he thought was Sarah. But when he opened it he saw an apparition of a woman dressed in old-fashioned clothing. She looked like Sarah but she was crying and calling for someone and then she was gone.

"I don't think I can go back into that room Sarah. Is there another place I can stay until tomorrow morning?"

"Sure Chaz you can sleep in another room."

Chaz was sure he wouldn't sleep for the rest of the night. Sarah tried to reassure him that it was simply his imagination getting the better of him after Hannah's stories of the crying banshees. But try as she might she couldn't convince herself that it was nothing for she'd dreamed of the same woman on the balcony wearing the exact same clothing that she'd found in the steamer trunk in the attic. Was the spirit of Evelyn Elizabeth really mourning the loss of her lover? Was Harrison House really haunted? Maybe

Haunted Heart / Laverne Stewart

Hannah's stories of her ancestor trying to reach out to her from beyond the grave were true?

Sarah refused to believe it was real. *This place is getting to me and so are Hannah's tall tales,* she thought.

Within a couple of hours Chaz was calm enough to go back to bed. The tea had helped to soothe him back to asleep once more. But in the morning, as soon as breakfast was over, he said he was heading home.

Sarah felt sad seeing her best friend leave but he promised he would call as soon as he arrived home. He hugged Hannah and, even though he wanted to give Patrick a squeeze, he shook his hand instead. Patrick then decided to have some fun and prove to Chaz that he wasn't homophobic. Not only did he give him a hug but he gave him an awkward and very hasty kiss on the cheek.

Sarah howled with laughter. It was the first time she'd ever seen Chaz shocked into silence and he left giggling like a little girl with a crush. It was also hilarious to see Patrick kissing a man after he'd clearly defined his masculinity and his preference for women this summer.

After Chaz had driven away Patrick and Sarah decided they needed to get back to work.

The following day the painters and wallpaper hangers moved on to the second floor.

By the next week they were working on the first floor. In a month they'd managed to finish every room in the house.

It was the end of August and everything that needed to be done was finished.

Haunted Heart / Laverne Stewart

Hannah, Patrick and Sarah walked through the entire mansion looking at the transformation that had been done in just twelve weeks. The home was ready for a real estate sign. Everything she wanted to donate to the museum had already been removed from the house. With these things gone the place looked far less cluttered.

Sarah had done a marvelous job of picking paint colors and wallpaper patterns.

Thanks to a lot of very long days and a lot of hard work by Patrick and his restoration team, Harrison House was the magnificent place it had once been.

Sarah decided it would appeal to more home buyers if she left all of the furniture where it was until the home was sold. Only then would she ask Tim Isaac Auctioneers to collect all of it and sell it for her.

With all of the work finished, Sarah decided she would remain here for just a few more days and then she would return to Boston.

When she told Patrick and Hannah about her decision to leave Harrison House, Hannah became very quiet.

This elderly woman was never at a loss for words., and Sarah had expected Hannah to chastise her. When the old woman simply turned and walked away without a word, Sarah felt the sharp pain of guilt stab at her conscience.

Patrick however was not reserved in his opinion of what she was about to do.

19

Patrick was visibly angry on hearing Sarah voice her plans to sell Harrison House and move to Boston. "You're making a huge mistake," he told her. "Harrison House is a part of who you are whether you want it to be or not."

He slammed his fist down on the dining table. "You see this? Generations of Harrisons sat here. Hell, you ate here when you were a kid and you've sat at this table with Hannah and me over the past three months. I have poured my heart and soul into this place. This has meaning to me. I had hoped, in time, while you were working beside me on this place, that it would come to have meaning to you too. I thought you would start to care about something other than selling everything and going back to Boston. I can't see why you'd want to give up what you have here for a stupid job in a restaurant and a rented apartment."

"You're right Patrick I have a huge, beautifully restored property. Thanks to my contractor the job has been completed on time and on budget. What I decide to do is my business and hardly the place of my employee to give his two cents worth."

She reached into her purse and pulled out an envelope. Patrick opened it. Inside was a bank draft for $100,000.

"I have paid you for your services what more do you want from me?"

Sarah knew she sounded like a real bitch. She was angry with him and she wanted him to get angry with her too. She wanted him to beg her to stay. She needed him to tell her he loved her and couldn't bear to see her go. He only needed to say three little words. 'Please don't go' or 'I love you', either would have convinced her to remain. But he became very quiet.

Perhaps, she thought, *he was relieved the job was finished and now that he had the bank draft she'd given him in payment for the work, he would be glad to be rid of her so he could go on to new adventures and new women. Patrick had shared her bed these past few months but he never told her he wanted to share the rest of his life with her. For him, it had been nothing more than a job with fringe benefits. He got paid to play after hours with the boss. Well to hell with him and to hell with Harrison House.*

"Thanks. It was fun while it lasted, eh Red?"

"Yeah, it sure was stud. I'm sure with all of your assets you won't find it hard to find another lady who needs your services."

Patrick reached out and grabbed Sarah by the arm. He pulled her close and kissed her long and hard. "That's just a little taste of what you're leaving behind lady."

"Go to hell Patrick Gallagher."

"Too late; I'm already there."

Patrick pushed her away, turned his back on her and walked out of the dining room. She refused to follow him but she knew he was gone when she heard the front door slam. Patrick got into his pick-up truck. He'd be damned if he was going to let her see him cry.

She went to her room and started throwing clothes into suitcases. Tears ran down her face. When she arrived here she couldn't wait to get the work over with and sell this place. Now that she'd invested so much of herself into it and since she'd fallen in love with him, the thought of selling it really didn't hold much appeal. She could hear her mother's voice in her head. 'Sarah please be practical. The job is over. So is the summer and this summertime affair. It's time to get back to reality. He doesn't love you. Sell the house and get back to Boston where you belong.'

She tried to quiet her mother's voice in her head because for the first time in her life, Sarah truly felt as though she belonged somewhere. This was where she wanted and needed to be. For the first time in her life Sarah felt as though she were home. Patrick and Chaz were right. She was making a huge mistake. But what was a single 25-year-old going to do with a massive property like this? She had no idea how to operate an inn.

Then she thought of old spinster Gertrude Harrison who'd lived here all alone. She wasn't going to end up like that. Patrick didn't love her. It was time to leave. She picked up the telephone and called the real estate agency.

Hannah kept herself busy. For the rest of the day she was pleasant but remaining quiet about the house sale. *Why wasn't Hannah trying to change her mind?*

Hannah told herself Sarah would come to her senses soon enough. She knew Patrick desperately wanted Sarah to stay. She knew beyond a doubt that he was in love with her. She could see them here together and happy if they would only stop being so stubborn and tell one another how they really felt.

Patrick wouldn't ask her to stay because he wanted it to be her decision to keep Harrison House and remain here. She hadn't told him she loved him so he said nothing about his feelings for her either. If she was determined to do this he couldn't stop her. But there was something he could do. He just needed enough time to make it happen.

A palpable feeling of sadness had fallen over Harrison House. Hannah had hardly set foot in the kitchen over the next two days. Patrick went back to his apartment and wouldn't answer his phone or email.

By the third day Sarah could see no reason to remain any longer. If and when there was an offer on the house, the real estate agent would call her in Boston to let her know. The next morning, just before Sarah was about to drive back to Boston, Hannah called Patrick.

"She's going. If you don't do something or say something to convince her to stay you're a stupid arse who deserves to be lonely and miserable for the rest of your life. Now get over here before it's too late."

Hannah hung up the phone. She needed to think of something quick to keep her here a while longer. What could she do? Then Marmalade, who'd jumped up on the counter next to the knife drawer, gave her an idea.

"Get down from there you bad thing. But here's a bit of chicken for helping me to find a way to buy some time."

About an hour later Sarah came down stairs with her luggage and carried the bags to the curb. She was about to put them in the trunk when she noticed all four of her tires had been slashed.

"Oh great! Wonderful! Now what am I supposed to do?"

She went back inside where she found Hannah sitting at the table with a cup of tea. She looked up and saw Sarah standing there with tears streaming down her face. "What's wrong girlie?"

"Someone's slashed all four of my tires. Even if I wanted to leave I can't now because there are no garages open on a Sunday to install new tires."

Hannah heard the words she was hoping to hear. "Sarah you said 'Even if you wanted to go.' Are you telling me you want to stay?"

Sarah started to cry. Hannah got up from the table and put her arms around Sarah and gave her a hug.

"And just who is saying you have to go anywhere? Harrison House is yours and I know you have fallen in love with the place. Why it shows in all of your hard work. You are trying very hard to be cool and calm around him because you are afraid of rejection. I was born at night my girlie but I wasn't born last night and that's for sure. You have fallen deeply in love with Patrick Gallagher. I told the pair of you that you were one another's destinies. You are meant to be here and you are meant to be with him. Give yourself permission to stay. Really girlie, I have only been to Boston once and indeed it is a nice place but who there loves you like I do and like Patrick does?"

"We slept together but that doesn't mean a thing. Never once did he say he loved me."

Hannah put her hand on Sarah's. "Did you tell him how you feel?"

"No."

Sarah wiped her eyes and sat down at the table. Hannah poured her a cup of tea. "Let me read the leaves once you are finished and that will tell the tale of what's to be done to be certain."

Haunted Heart / Laverne Stewart

Sarah and Hannah sat for a while sipping their tea in silence. Hannah could tell that Sarah was miserable but it wasn't her place to say anything about what needed to be said and done about that relationship. That would be up to Patrick and Sarah to figure out.

Sarah had invested herself in this house but more importantly she had given her heart to a man she wasn't sure loved her back. Life had taught her to be independent and she didn't want to take a chance on something that was far from certain. Unless Patrick was willing to tell her he loved her completely and that he wanted to make a life with her here, Sarah wouldn't be the first to leave herself open to be vulnerable and heartbroken. She felt it was better to part as friends than to hear 'It was fun while it lasted Red. Come back any time you feel like having some more fun.'

When the tea was finished Hannah took Sarah's cup. She looked and smiled. "The house will sell very quickly. The new owner will want to take possession immediately. Sarah you will not refuse the offer. It will simply be too good not to accept."

"Well there you have it Hannah. You said the leaves never lie. So it looks like I am meant to sell the place and move back to Boston after all. As soon as a tire shop is open tomorrow morning, I will have my car towed over there. When the new tires are installed I'll be on my way. I have a headache. I need to lie down."

Sarah went to her bedroom. She cried until no more tears would come and then she fell asleep. Soon she was dreaming again. *She was dressed in the white gown with emerald sash and green bonnet and gloves. She saw him standing on the other side of the ballroom. He was very handsome in his formal wear. They danced throughout the night to many waltzes. It was a wonderful, grand affair which included being presented to society as Miss Evelyn*

Haunted Heart / Laverne Stewart

Elizabeth Harrison. She was blissfully happy and then everything changed. She was crying now standing on the balcony. There were people standing in the street. There, beneath the carriage, lay his broken body. Sarah woke up in a sweat and she was screaming.

Hannah climbed the stairs to Sarah's bedroom as quickly as she could. "Dear God in heaven Sarah what's wrong?"

Sarah tried very hard to compose herself. When she was calm enough she told Hannah about the dream. "Evelyn is trying to tell you about the night her Padraig died."

"I read her diary. I know they had an affair and that he'd planned to ask her father's permission to marry her. But he died that night and three days later so did she. Hannah do you know what happened?"

Hannah nodded. "Yes girlie. I've seen that night many times in my dreams and visions since coming here to Harrison House. T'was a terrible night indeed. After the dance Padraig asked for a meeting with Cornelius Harrison. They went into the study and Padraig told him that he was in love with Evelyn and wanted permission to court her and marry her as soon as possible. Cornelius laughed and said it wasn't possible. He reminded Padraig that he was Catholic and they were Anglican. Also he told Padraig that an employee with no fortune and no way to keep his daughter in the lifestyle to which she had been raised and was accustomed to, would never be permitted to marry his daughter even if they were the same faith. Then he told him that even if he did have the same religion and wealth, he was too late in his request. He explained that his business partner at the shipyard had a son who'd already expressed an interest in Evelyn and that he'd given his permission for Gerald Pugh to court his daughter. Then Padraig broke the news that Evelyn was expecting his child. Cornelius Harrison was livid. He ordered Padraig out of his house and

Haunted Heart / Laverne Stewart

off the property immediately. Padraig tried to tell the older man how much they were in love and that he would work hard to regain his family's fortune but old Cornelius would listen to none of what Padraig had to say. Padraig left the house and went out to the stables to gather his things. He was about to leave when the old man came out on to the street with a rifle in his hands. He pointed it at Patrick and he told him he would call the police if he ever stepped foot on his property again. Then he fired a shot. Evelyn had been waiting up stairs in her room. She screamed as she saw her father with the loaded gun pointed at Padraig. The bullet missed but the sound of the gunfire startled a team of horses in the street hitched to a carriage that belonged to a couple who'd come to the ball. Padraig tried to jump out of the way but he was too close to the horses and they trampled him. His neck was broken. He'd been killed instantly. Evelyn saw it all and was hysterical. That night she suffered a miscarriage. With her man dead and next, the miscarriage, she was inconsolable. The doctor prescribed laudanum to calm her nerves. She remained in her bed for the next three days. The morning her body was discovered the entire contents of the laudanum bottle was gone. They said she died of an overdose but I believe she died of a broken heart. She simply chose to use the laudanum to leave this world so she could be with the man she loved."

Sarah was crying. Such a sad, horrible end to such a beautiful romance.

"Sarah she's been trying to tell you her story your whole life. She's been talking to you in your dreams and even in certain ways while you've been awake since you've been here. Through you and Patrick the wrong that was done all those years ago will be made right. You will have the love and the life that was denied to her and Padraig."

Haunted Heart / Laverne Stewart

Sarah didn't see how this was possible. She was returning to Boston. "That's not going to happen Hannah. You said yourself the house was going to sell quickly."

Hannah smiled. "We shall see what we shall see. All will be well in the end. Of this I am certain. Remember the other time I read your tea leaves? I saw a marriage in the garden and a baby."

Sarah shook her head. 'No you are mixing things up. I read in Evelyn's diary that her dream was to have a garden wedding. What you were seeing was her desire to marry Padraig and the baby you saw was his baby that she had miscarried. That's all it was and nothing more."

"We shall see what we shall see girlie."

Patrick still hadn't shown up. *Damn that foolish, stubborn boy,* Hannah thought. *What was keeping him? Pride? The fear of rejection? He should know that she loved him as much as he loved her. But neither wanted to allow themselves to be vulnerable in case the answer was no. Neither wanted to risk a broken heart. But nothing in this world that is worth anything of value comes without a risk.*

Hannah could only pray that he was doing something that involved a risk if it meant finding a way to keep her here with him; with them. Her sense of things told her indeed he was. She just hoped he would be here with something that would convince her that staying here was worth her risk of allowing herself to feel what she'd been denying these past three months. *They were one another's destinies and nothing and no one else would satisfy either them or those who left this world too soon to see their own love and lives fulfilled. Evelyn Elizabeth Harrison would not rest until that which had been denied her and Padraig was fulfilled in Sarah and Patrick.*

Haunted Heart / Laverne Stewart

Sarah decided she needed to escape this place for a while so she could think. She put on her sneakers. "Hannah I need to get some fresh air and I think a walk will help clear my head. I'll be back in about an hour."

"Okay girlie. Be careful. I'll have lunch ready by the time you return."

It wasn't five minutes after Sarah was gone that the telephone rang. Patrick called to say he was sorry they'd argued and to ask her not to go and that he had something he needed to tell her.

"She's gone for a walk boy-o. Someone with a big old knife slashed her tires so you've got until about 11 o'clock tomorrow until she's able to leave, so whatever you've got planned you'd better do it quick."

"I'll be over as soon as I can."

When Hannah hung up the phone she went back to the kitchen sink where she was washing a butcher knife. "Marmalade this neighbourhood is really going down hill. Imagine someone slashing that girl's tires just as she was about to leave. What's the world coming to?"

Sarah walked into the city's centre and back again.

She felt revitalized. She knew her life in Boston was going nowhere. Chaz was right, what did she really have there? A job as a server in an upscale eatery and some night courses in interior design wasn't much to write home about and even if she did write that letter, there was no family to receive her news.

Harrison House had become home to her over the past three months. Hannah was the kind of mother she'd always wished for.

As for Patrick, well, it might have only been a summertime fling to him, but it was something she would cherish always. He might not have fallen deeply in love the way she did, but she'd get over it.

She would go back to Boston. Maybe someday there would be someone that would love her enough to want to share their life with her.

When she arrived home she found the realtor waiting for her in the kitchen having a cup of tea with Hannah. There was a contract on the table. All she had to do was sign the papers and the home would be listed immediately.

Sarah looked at the contract. She could decide not to sell this place and stay here but being here and knowing Patrick didn't love her would be too much to bear. Sarah reached for the pen.

Hannah reached out and placed her hand over Sarah's "Are you absolutely sure you want to sell Harrison House?"

Sarah knew she was making a mistake but she couldn't stand to be here without him. "It's the only way Hannah. Without him I would ramble around in this house like a ghost. Sarah laughed at the irony.

"Evelyn Elizabeth has haunted this place for 167 years. If I stay here, I would be like a dead woman and it would feel like an eternity without him."

Sarah signed all of the necessary paperwork.

The realtor shook her hand and said as soon as there were purchase offers she would be in touch.

Haunted Heart / Laverne Stewart

The realtor looked thrilled. Sarah was devastaed. All she wanted to do now was to get her tires replaced and go back to Boston.

Hannah had placed her lunch on the table but Sarah didn't feel like eating.

For the rest of the day she moped around the house and walked the property.

What was she doing? She was selling off her family's heritage. She should have told Patrick how she felt. What stopped her? It was her fear of rejection.

Sarah felt as though she couldn't breathe.

As she walked along the rock wall she thought of the love between Padraig and Evelyn Elizabeth. Their love wasn't served then.

Hannah was wrong when she said that she and Patrick were one another's destinies. It looked like Evelyn Elizabeth would never rest in peace.

20

The rest of the evening and into the night Sarah felt so alone. She couldn't wait to escape this place. Harrison House was now a sad reminder of what could have been but wasn't for both Evelyn and her.

She looked up at Evelyn Elizabeth's portrait. Of all of the portraits in Harrison House this was the only one that didn't frighten her. "Too bad things didn't work out huh Evie?"

Sarah slept but not soundly. She woke the next morning and looked at the clock. It was 7 a.m. In an hour her car would have new tires installed. She could be on the road by 8:30. She dressed and packed. Then she wrote a note to Hannah.

Dear Hannah

I couldn't bear to see your face as I said goodbye. So, by the time you see this, I will likely be across the border in Maine. Thank you for all of your kindness to me this summer. I will call you when I get back to Boston tonight.

Love,

Sarah.

She slowly walked through the old house taking a last look at the walls with their portraits that once frightenened her so badly. She heard the creaks in the wooden floor boards.

She marveled at the transformation that had been done to bring this grand old mansion back to life.

Harrison House would soon make another owner very happy. She carried her bags to the curb where a taxi was waiting. Within 20 minutes she was paying for the newly installed tires and she was driving over the Saint John harbor bridge unable to see the water below because of the heavy Bay of Fundy fog.

An hour later, as Hannah was dusting the mahogany table in the foyer, she saw Sarah's note. Her eyes became watery. She reached for her hankerchief that she kept in the pocket of her apron and wiped her eyes.

The door opened. Patrick ran into the room calling "Sarah, Sarah!"

"It's too late boy-o. She gone. Left 90 minutes ago. By now she's in Maine on her way back to Boston. I told you to be here early. What's kept you?"

"I was at the realtors. I just bought this place. I wanted to come here to tell her that I didn't want some stranger buying it. I wanted to tell her that I want to make a home for us here and that I want her to be my wife. Things took longer than I'd thought …"

He slumped down into a wing-back chair and put his head in his hands.

"Well my boy, the only thing I can tell you is to go after her."

"I don't think it will do much good Hannah. She doesn't love me. If she did she'd have stayed."

"Did you ever give her any reason to think you loved her? Did you tell her how you feel?"

"No."

"Why not?"

"I thought she was only interested in a fling. She said it was a casual thing. A bit of fun and that it would be over when the renovations were done. Sure enough, she's gone like she said she would be once the house was ready for sale."

"I love you Patrick but you are one daft buggar. She's gone because you never let her know you love her. She never told you how she feels because she was afraid of rejection. Unlike you Patrick, who always had the love of your mother and father, God rest his soul, and me for that matter, she grew up in a house where there was little love shown. She is insecure about sharing her deepest feelings. Make no mistake Patrick, she loves you. I know this as sure as there is breath in my body. Go to her Patrick and get down on your knees and tell her you love her and need her to come home."

Patrick hugged Hannah.

"I've got to stick around for a couple of more days but, by Wednesday, I will be going to her. I just hope she doesn't say no."

"Anything worth something in life comes with a bit of risk. Take a chance boy-o. I have a feeling all will work out in the end."

By suppertime that night Hannah was back in Boston. She walked into the apartment, which once felt cozy, but now felt suffocating after the summer in the spacious mansion.

As promised she called Hannah. She heard the old woman's voice.

"Leave a message. I'll get back to you as soon as I can."

"Hannah, it's Sarah. I arrived safely. Traffic wasn't too heavy. I am so tired. I miss you. I miss ... I miss...never mind. I will call you later. Bye."

She looked around. She didn't want to be here. She picked up the phone and dialed Chaz's number.

"Hellooooo!"

"Hi Chaz, I'm back."

"Darling! Oh how I've missed you! We have so much to catch up on. I need to tell you about the guy I met and what's happening at work. Girl, there is so much drama in the kitchen! The sous-chef threw a pot at the head chef and then quit and that left the kitchen backed up and we were scrambling that night and we're still trying to keep up with him gone.

Sarah, you know I love you but girl, why did you come back here? You know with that gorgeous house and that even more gorgeous guy, I sure as hell would not be coming back to Bean Town, a tiny apartment and a server's job even if it is at a five-star restauant."

"Chaz, I couldn't stay."

"Why not?"

"The house renovations are done. It's now for sale and the summer romance was just that. A summer fling. He never gave me any hint that he felt anything more for me than someone to have some fun with."

Haunted Heart / Laverne Stewart

"Do you love him?"

"Yes."

"Did you tell him?"

"No."

"Oh, of course you didn't. I knew better than to even ask. Sometimes you've got to take a risk and stop being worried about rejection. Listen, what you need is Gone With the Wind and cheesecake. My place. Now. Get your ass over here girl."

"Chaz I am so tired but I just can't stand to be here in this place, alone. I will be there in half an hour."

She hung up the phone and then took a shower and got dressed. The low mood she was in was eased somewhat as soon as she got to his place and Chaz started reciting the dialogue of all of the characters.

"After all, tomorrow is another day," he said in his best Miss Scarlet impression. He looked at Sarah in hopes of wild applause. She was curled up in a ball and asleep on the sofa.

"Poor you!"

He pulled a blanket over her and then turned out the lights.

In the morning Sarah woke to the smell of bacon and eggs. It should have made her hungry. Not this morning. Instead she was feeling nausated. Must have been the cheesecake, she thought.

She got up and went to the kitchen. "None for me thanks."

"Coffee?"

"Nope. Not feeling well. I am going home. I've got to get groceries, do laundry and hopefully convince Sam to give me a job back at the restaurant."

"You only have to ask darling. He's been complaining all summer that you were the best server the restaurant had and the rest of us need to be more like you. Call me later darling."

Chaz gave her a hug and waved as she walked to her car that was parked on the sidewalk in front of his apartment building.

Sarah went to the store to get some food and then went home where she put it in the refrigerator and pantry and then unpacked her suitcases. She spent the rest of the morning doing laundry. By noon the restaurant would be open. She called Sam, the restaurant's front of house manager.

"Sarah, I am so happy you're back. We need you. Are you available tonight?"

"Yes."

"Great! See you before the supper shift."

Sarah spent the rest of the afternoon getting settled back in her apartment which no longer felt like home. It was just a place. Home, she now knew, was with Hannah and Marmalade. Home was where she wished she could be with Patrick.

By 3:30 she was dressed in a white linen blouse and black pants. Standard uniform of the Green Onion. She lived just a block away from the restaurant and was there in plenty of time to chat with some co-workers before dinner service started at 4 p.m. The restaurant was unusually busy for a

Tuesday night. Business suppers filled the dining area. By 10 p.m. the last of the dinner guests had departed and the staff got to work with the cleanup.

She was back home by midnight. A shower removed the smell of the supper menu from her hair and she slipped into a nightgown and then into bed.

Soon she was dreaming. *Evelyn Elizabeth and Padraig were there with her.*

"Don't let your fears keep you from your future. Go to him Sarah. Tell him how you feel."

Sarah woke. The clock on her bedside table said 1:11 a.m. She was unable to go back to sleep as she lay there thinking about the dream and about Patrick.

"If only it were that easy."

Eventually she fell back to sleep. She woke suddenly with an urge to vomit. She just made it to the bathroom and dropped to her knees and retched. The nausea continued throughout the morning. Chaz called. "Girl, you sound awful. What's wrong?"

"Sick."

"What kind of sick?"

"Stomach."

"Two mornings in a row. Are you pregnant?"

"Chaz, no! Of course not."

"Are you sure?"

"We were careful."

"Only one way to know for sure. Go get one of those home pregnancy kits from the pharmacy."

"Chaz! I don't need to. I'm not pregnant. Goodbye you sweet man. I love you."

"Bye darling!"

The next morning, as Sarah was power puking in the toilet, she thought Chaz might be right. Pregnant. God no! When she was able to get dressed and drive, she went to a pharmacy at the nearest mall and bought a testing kit.

She took it home and peed on the stick. She waited. Two blue lines. Postive.

She sat on the cold tile bathroom floor staring at those two blue lines that were the signal that her life was about to change when the phone rang.

She only became aware of the phone on the third ring and ran to the livingroom to pick up. "Hello?"

"Well now girlie. You've had a shock and that's for sure."

"What are you talking about Hannah?"

"That wee babe that will be here in about seven months."

"Hannah how do you know this? I only just found out myself ten minutes ago."

"Evelyn and I have been having a chat this morning and she told me the baby will be here by next spring."

"Oh Hannah," Sarah said as she started to cry so hard she could barely draw a breath.

"There, there now girlie. Everything is going to be okay. You just need to come back home and let old Hannah look after you. And didn't I tell you there was going to be a wedding in the garden this fall and a baby on the way? Sure enough the tea leaves never lie."

Hannah's prediction was only half true.

"Baby, yes. Wedding, no."

"Well there will be once you tell Patrick."

"I'm not going to tell him."

"Why not? He's the daddy. He has a right to know."

"I don't want him to feel obligated. I can handle things on my own. There are plenty of mothers who do this alone."

"You have to tell him Sarah. It's only right."

"A baby is no reason for a marriage. I want to marry a man who loves me."

"He does Sarah."

"He never told me. Never even hinted at it."

"Did you give him any encouragement?"

"No."

"You didn't tell him you loved him either. Oh for goodness sake you two are a fine pair. Well you can tell him yourself when you see him."

"See him?"

Haunted Heart / Laverne Stewart

"I told him to go after you and bring you home. He's leaving first thing tomorrow morning. Now don't be proud Sarah. Tell him you love him. Pack your bags and come home."

"Hannah why are you pushing him like this? If he wanted me to stay he would have said something before I left."

"I'll say no more but maybe with a little help from Evelyn Elizabeth and Padraig, the two of you will start to see that you are meant to be together."

"You know I don't believe they are reaching out from the other side Hannah."

"Think what you will Sarah but I know what I know."

Sure enough both Sarah and Patrick were visited in their sleep that night with Patrick learning what Sarah already new.

21

Patrick woke in a cold sweat. The vivid dream was coming back to him with clarity. A baby girl with red copper curls wrapped in a flannel blanket was being handed to him by a nurse and Sarah was laying nearby in a hospital bed. Partick sat at the edge of his bed.

"Is this real? Are Hannah's predictions of a wedding and a baby really true?"

Patrick could no longer sleep. At 3 a.m. he decided now was as good a time as any to make the drive to Boston. An hour later he crossed the U.S.-Canada border at the Calais, Maine border area.

"It's a little early to be entering the U.S. isn't it son? Where are you from?"

"Saint John."

"Where are you headed?"

"Boston."

"What's the purpose of your visit?"

"My baby's mother lives there. I am going to ask her to marry me and to come back to Canada."

"You got a ring yet?"

"No. It's a spur of the moment decision."

"Well, I always was a sucker for romance. Go get your bride man!"

"Thanks!"

By 5:30 Patrick was nearing Bangor. He estimated he should make it to Boston before 10:30.

He made good time. Using his truck's GPS he had no trouble finding the address for Sarah's apartment that Hannah had given him. He parked in front of the brownstone building and then ran to the front door. He opened the foyer and saw a panel with apartment numbers.

He pressed the number of her apartment on the intercom. He waited. She wasn't home. "Damn." He went to the Green Onion. It was closed but he could see Chaz inside and knocked on the window.

Chaz saw him and waved. "Well hello there you! What brings you to Boston? No wait, don't tell me. I know. You just couldn't stand the thought of not seeing me again right? Kidding! She's not here Patrick. Sorry."

"Do you have any idea where she might be?"

"Doctor's appointment. She's not been feeling well."

"What's wrong."

"Nope. Not telling," Chaz made a zipper motion across his mouth. "She should be home in about an hour though. I'd wait for her there if I were you."

"Just tell me if it's serious."

"Nope, sorry. I like gossip but this isn't my drama so I'll just be quiet from backstage."

Patrick was tired and getting iritated. He got back in his truck and returned to Sarah's apartment where he sat on brick-colored sandstone front steps.

By noon he saw Sarah's convertible coming down the street. She didn't notice him until she had parked and got out of the car and was walking toward the building.

"Hannah told me you were coming."

"Hello Sarah."

"Chaz told me you were at the doctor's. Are you pregnant?"

"Chaz has a big mouth."

"Are you pregnant, Sarah?"

Patrick had placed a hand on her upper arm and drew her close and looked into her eyes.

"Tell me."

"Yes."

"Why didn't you call me?"

"I didn't think you would want to know."

"I wouldn't want to know that I am going to be a father? Is that what you think of me? 'Love em and leave em' is that how you have me pegged? Well it seems to me that you're the one who deserves that title. You took off without even saying as much as goodbye. Why didn't you tell me you were pregnant?"

"I have a right to privacy."

Haunted Heart / Laverne Stewart

"That baby is mine too. I have a right to know."

"Well I didn't think you'd care. We had a summer fling. We agreed to that. Remember?"

"Well it was more than that to me. And now you're pregnant."

"So?"

"So marry me Sarah."

"No."

"No? Why not?"

"Because a baby is no reason to get married."

"You are the most stubborn, independent woman I have ever met, you know that Red?"

"Yeah, independent enough that I don't need you crossing over the border to come rescue me and take me back there."

"And what do you think you're going to do? Raise the baby by yourself in this place?"

"What's wrong with this place?"

"It's not a home. It's not your home. Your home is back in Saint John with Hannah and me. If you'll have me."

"With you? In Harrison House? Are you asking me to marry you so you can have that place? I know how much you don't want it sold."

"You know what Sarah? To hell with you."

Haunted Heart / Laverne Stewart

Sarah knew she had gone too far but her temper had gotten the better of her.

"Patrick wait. I'm sorry."

Her apology went unheard. By now he was back in his truck and had started the engine. The screech of his tires and the smell of burning rubber was the response she got as he raced away.

Why hadn't she told him she loved him? He never said it either. Maybe he was asking to marry her out of a sense of duty. Maybe Hannah and his mother had talked him into it.

"Well there will be no fall wedding in the garden now. Sorry Hannah to spoil the wedding plans," Sarah said as she slowly climbed the stairs to her second floor apartment.

Patrick wasn't sure what to do next. He was too tired to drive back to Saint John. He would get a hotel and sleep. But first he wanted to get drunk.

Patrick wasn't much of a drinker but if there was any time to drown one's sorrows this was it. He went back to the Green Onion which was, by now, serving lunch. Not interested in eating he went straight to the bar and ordered a bottle of whiskey and a shot glass.

By the time he'd swallowed his second shot, Chaz saw him sitting there looking defeated.

"She told you?"

"Yeah."

"You don't look so good. Things didn't go so well?"

"No shit Sherlock," Patrick said as he knocked back his third shot. By now he was starting to slur his words.

Haunted Heart / Laverne Stewart

"Look, Patrick. You're a nice guy and this is a nice place. Why don't I call you a cab?"

"No thanks, Chaz. I'm good. Peachy keen," he said as he swallowed another round.

"I'm serious Patrick. You can get shitfaced if you want but not here. Come on. Come with me." "Sam, I am clocking out for a bit. Got to take Romeo some place where he can sleep it off."

Chaz helped Patrick to his feet and walked him to the front door.

"Where are your keys?"

Patrick reached in his pocket and tossed them at Chaz. When Chaz had Patrick buckled in, he got behind the wheel and started the truck.

"It's been a while but I think I remember how," he said as he pulled away from the curb.

"Where are you taking me?"

"Home, to my place."

"Are you hitting on me?"

"Honey, you are my type but I love Sarah and would never try to steal her man."

"I'm not her man."

"Well you could be if you tried a little harder. All you need to do is tell her you love her. Three little words 'I love you' is all that stands between you and the girl of your dreams. Darling when you sober up tomorrow you're going to march that cute little butt of yours over to Sarah's place.

You're going to tell her you're sorry. You're going to tell her you love her and you're going to ask her to marry you like a gentleman would do. Get down on one knee with a ring and some flowers."

Chaz was proud of the speech he just gave. He looked over at Patrick but the man was slumped over in the passenger seat and was starting to snore.

"Oh, my God. You're a hot mess!"

It was all Chaz could do to get Patrick out of the truck and up three flights of stairs to his apartment. He put him on his sofa and covered him with a blanket.

"Gotta go. I will be back after my shift is over. Behave yourself."

Patrick was snoring like a chainsaw. "Nothing to worry about. You're clearly not going anywhere," Chaz said as he closed the apartment door.

By 8 p.m. Patrick awoke and looked around. He wasn't sure where he was but he did remember Chaz helping him into the apartment.

"Oh, look who's awake."

"Not so loud," Patrick said as he put his head in his hands.

"Here. Take these." Chaz handed him some Advil. "Hungry?"

"Nope."

"What happened with you and Sarah today?"

"She's pregnant. But you already knew that. I asked her to marry me. She said no."

"That's because you forgot the most important part of the proposal."

"I did?"

"I tried to explain in the truck but you were too stupid with whiskey to hear me. I said all you need to do is tell her you love her. Three little words 'I love you' is all that stands between you and the girl of your dreams. You're going to tell her your sorry. You're going to ask her to marry you like a gentleman. Get down on one knee with a ring and some flowers."

The phone rang.

"Hello. May I speak to Chaz Alvarez please?"

"Speaking."

"This is Tufts Medical Center."

"Yes?"

"Sarah Jane Harrison has you listed as her next of kin. She's been admitted and is asking for you."

"Oh my God, is she okay?"

"She was admitted about an hour ago. I am not permitted to discuss her medical condition. You will have to get that information from the admitting physician."

"Thanks," Chaz said as he hung up the phone.

"It's Sarah. She's in the hospital. Let's go!"

Chaz and Patrick arrived at the information desk and were directed to the third floor. At the nursing station they were met by Dr. Paul Jensen. "Mr. Alvarez?"

"Yes."

The doctor then looked at Patrick. "And you are?"

"That's Sarah's fiance."

"She's going to be fine. She arrived at the emergency department complaining of cramping. We have done an ultasound and the baby is completely fine. Nothing to worry about. Cramping sometimes happens during a pregnancy. But in Sarah's case she should be okay. This appears to be a healthy and viable pregnancy. She's just entering her eighth week. We're going to keep her for observation overnight but I would say she should be good to go home tomorrow morning."

Chaz and Patrick thanked the doctor who told them it was okay to visit her in her room.

"Come on," Chaz said.

"No, you go ahead. Just tell her I was here."

"Why don't you want to see her?"

"I can't right now. Maybe in the morning."

Patrick was struggling to hold himself together and not break down in the hospital hallway.

As Patrick left he wondered why more straight men couldn't let people see their vulnerabilities.

"He loves her," he said with a smile and then walked into Sarah's room. She had some surprises in store for her tomorrow but Chaz wasn't about to give them away.

22

Just after breakfast Sarah was discharged from the hospital.

The doctor told her that being on her feet for hours and carrying heavy trays of food might not be a good idea given the cramping she'd just experinced.

He told her and Chaz that she needed to rest. "Time with your feet up would be advisable. Be sure your young man takes good care of you."

"Oh no worries doctor. We will make sure she does just that. Come on. Let's get you out of here."

They drove back to Sarah's apartment. Chaz helped Sarah to the second floor and unlocked the door for her.

"Sarah I am going to leave you to rest. Call me later?"

"You sure you won't come in?"

"Positive. Later darling."

Sarah stepped inside the apartment. There, sitting in the living room, was Patrick.

"What are you doing here?"

"I came to apologize for the way I behaved yesterday."

"I'm sorry too."

"Sarah, I came her to ask you to come home. Not because you're pregnant. I want you to come home with me because I miss you. I need you in my life. Nothing is good in my life without you. And most important of all, I love you."

Patrick took the five steps from the sofa to where she stood and then got down on one knee. He pulled a box from his pocket and opened it. Inside was a large, yet not ostentatious diamond ring. "Will you marry me Sarah?"

Sarah felt a lump in her throat and tears stinging her eyes. She was unable to speak but managed to nod. He stood up and took her in his arms.

As they kissed, Chaz, who'd been listening from the other side of the apartment door, did a happy dance all the way through the hallway, down the stairs and into the street.

Hannah, some 800 kilometres away, smiled and sipped her tea at the same moment. "Fall wedding it is then. Told you Evelyn Elizabeth. The tea leaves have never failed me yet."

Haunted Heart / Laverne Stewart

23

Sarah packed her bags and handed them to Patrick, who loaded them into his truck.

Chaz arrived to hug them both and wish them a safe trip back to Saint John.

"I'll call you when we get there," she said.

"Love you Sarah. Love you too Patrick," Chaz said as he waved goodbye. A September wedding. Garden weddings are so beautiful. He could hardly wait for the day. Chaz was to be the master of honour who would walk her down the isle.

Patrick gripped the steering whieel, and with Sarah beside him, threw his truck into drive. They made it home just after 10 p.m. and Sarah could hardly keep her eyes open.

Patrick helped her up the front steps and into Harrison House.

Hannah was waiting and hugged them both. She told Patrick he needed some sleep and promised she would see Sarah to bed.

Patrick kissed Sarah and said he'd see her in the morning.

"You're not staying?"

"Can't. I have a meeting at the bank first thing. I will be over as soon as I can. Goodnight, love."

"Goodnight Patrick," she said as she kissed him and then allowed Hannah to help her up to her third-floor bedroom.

Haunted Heart / Laverne Stewart

Minutes after she had changed into a nightgown and was in bed, she was sound asleep.

"Goodnight girlie. Sleep well my dear," the old lady said.

The sound of hammering was coming from the front of the house. What was someone making all of that noise for? She went to the bedroom window and looked out. There on the front lawn was the real estate agent hammering a sold sign into the grass. Patrick was standing beside her. He shook her hand. *Why was Patrick shaking her hand?*

Sarah dressed quickly and ran from her bedroom down the hallway and to the front door. She opened it just as Patrick was about to put a key in the front door.

"Hello Sarah."

"Patrick why were you shaking that realtor's hand?

"That's what one usually does after one signs a deal and is handed a set of keys to one's new property."

"What do you mean one's new property?"

"Sarah, you sold Harrison House to me. I wanted to add a condition to the sales agreement but the realtor told me it wasn't something she could do anything about. She told me I'd have to ask you if you'd agree to the extra condition.

"What's that?"

"Not only do I want the contents of the home to remain with the estate – I really want the former owner to promise we'll be as happy when we're old and gray as we are now."

"I promise," she said as they kissed without reservation. He held her as though he would never let her go. Then the sound of a familiar and very loved sarcastic voice brought them back from their private world that only had room for two.

"Well if you two can come up for air, why don't you come into the kitchen. I have been saving something for this special occasion."

Patrick and Sarah held hands and they walked down the hall toward the kitchen. When they arrived they saw that Hannah had poured two glasses of sparking wine and one glass of grape juice. She handed the wine to Patrick and the non-alcoholic beverage to Sarah.

"Now drink your grape juice Sarah. It's full of vitamin C and antioxidants – wonderful for both you and the baby."

As the young couple downed their drinks, Hannah contined: "I'm told by Evelyn and Padraig that the baby's name will be Evelyn Elizabeth Hannah Gallagher and that I am to be her Godmother. Patrick, the renovations to Harrison House aren't quiet finished. The bedroom adjoining Sarah's will need to be turned into a nursery. I think pale green and yellow are lovely baby colors don't you? And Evie says there's not much time to plan for a garden wedding. Once you decide on the date we'll call Father O'Shanahan and book him for the ceremony."

"And don't worry about the reception," Hannah added. "I've got that all figured out. Sarah, you'll need to start thinking about your wedding dress immediately. Good God in heaven isn't this a turn of events? Now Sarah what was that you said about my tea leaves? Didn't I tell you there would be a wedding in the garden and a baby on the way?"

Sarah looked down at her stomach and then at a smiling Hannah and finally at Patrick. She came to Harrison House to get rid of the old place. She never would have imagined that in coming here she would find herself and her future.

Haunted Heart / Laverne Stewart

"I don't mean to pry Patrick but how is it possible that you can afford to buy this estate?" Sarah asked. "When you doubled the price of the place with the inclusion of the furniture that means you paid two million."

Patrick smiled. "Since I was eighteen, I've been investing my money in real estate. I fix houses up and flip them. I've done really well over the past seventeen years. When I learned you planned to sell this place after it was restored, I couldn't stand to see it go to anyone else. Harrison House is an historic treasure. I decided it was time to invest in a property where I could put down roots. It was my hope that when the work on this place was finished, you would be so madly in love with me you wouldn't want to leave. When you decided to sell the place and return to Boston I was devastated. I thought maybe you'd change your mind. But when you listed it for sale I knew I couldn't allow someone else to have it… I love you Sarah Jane Harrison."

"And I love you Patrick Ryan Gallagher."

They kissed again. The scent of wild flowers filled the air.

Hannah silently slipped out the back door, and went to her apartment where she sat in her rocker and smiled.

"Now didn't I tell you that all would be fine? Sarah came here. Harrison House has been restored. Those two young people have fallen in love and are to be married. And, in about seven months from now, there will be a wee one here with your name… My but you were the impatient one. I told you things would be fine and they are. Soon there will be a wedding and a baby shower and won't that be wonderful? … Why of course you can be there and of course you should be. You should have had a wedding and it should have been in the garden. Now you will see one there as you always wished for… You're right Evelyn. It's a happy day indeed."

24

A couple of days before the wedding Chaz arrived to help Sarah and Hannah with the preparations.

The sun broke through the fog shortly after 10 o'clock the morning of Sarah and Patrick's wedding. She woke early to start getting ready. As soon as she knew she was going to be married, Sarah worried about what she was going to wear. How was she going to find a dress on time? But Hannah had an idea.

"What if, with a few adjustments, you wore Evelyn Elizabeth's dress with the green satin sash?"

Sarah said she thought it had gone to the museum with the rest of the clothing and other things she'd donated.

Hannah smiled. "I asked Patrick not to send it. I had a feeling you'd have need of it for some reason."

Sarah made a face. She didn't like the idea of wearing a dress that a dead girl had worn.

"Ah, now don't be like that Sarah. Evelyn Elizabeth would be very pleased for you to wear her dress. It's a beautiful gown. I know it's old fashioned, but Patrick's mother is an excellent seamstress and I know she could redesign it into something amazing."

Eileen Gallagher was more talented than Hannah had said. After Sarah and Patrick's mother looked at a couple of dress styles that Sarah liked, she promised to have the dress remade in time for the wedding. The day before the wedding she arrived at Harrison House with the dress for the final fitting. When Eileen Gallagher took the dress out of the garment bag, Hannah, Chaz and Sarah were in awe.

"It's absolutely fabulous Sarah. Look at it. Go ahead, try it on!" Chaz insisted.

The gown was beautiful on the hanger but it was even more so with Sarah in it.

"Eileen Gallagher you have outdone yourself," Hannah said.

Indeed she had. The dress had been transformed into one that any bride would have been proud to wear. The once formal ball gown with a billowing skirt and long sleeves was no more. It was now sleeveless, and form-fitting. The green satin sash that cascaded down the back of the dress emphasized her narrow waist. It was a modern wedding gown for a modern woman and Sarah was thrilled. She hugged Patrick's mother and her tears said everything in that moment.

By 2 o'clock it was time to go into the garden where some 50 guests were seated, most of whom were relatives of the Gallaghers plus a few of Sarah's friends who had made the drive from Boston. Chaz squeezed her hand as he prepared to walk her down the isle and stand by her side as her attendant.

Father O'Shanahan welcomed everyone as a violinist played the wedding march. All eyes were on Sarah as she and Chaz walked from the mansion and into the garden, down a long red carpet.

Patrick could hardly breathe as he watched this woman he loved join him under the gazebo where he and his best man stood along with the priest. Patrick and Sarah looked into one another's eyes.

This is a moment most girls dream of all their lives she thought and look at me here now with this man. His sapphire eyes looking into the colour of hers that matched the sash on her dress. Sarah thought, *this is perfect. This is the start of the rest of our lives. What did I do to deserve all of this?*

The guests laughed as Sarah came back to earth when Father O'Shannahan said her name twice.

"Sarah? Sarah are you ready to say your vows?"

Sarah blushed and nodded.

"I, Sarah Jane Harrison, take you Patrick Ryan Gallagher, to be my husband, to have and to hold from this day forward, for better or for worse, for richer, for poorer, in sickness and in health, to love and to cherish; from this day forward until death do us part."

"I, Patrick Ryan Gallagher, take you, Sarah Jane Harrison, to be my lawfully wedded wife, my constant friend, my faithful partner and my love from this day forward. In the presence of God, our family and friends, I offer you my solemn vow to be your faithful partner in sickness and in health, in good times and in bad, and in joy as well as in sorrow. I promise to love you unconditionally, to support you in your goals, to honor and respect you, to laugh with you and cry with you, and to cherish you for as long as we both shall live."

"In the presence of God and these witnesses I now pronounce you, Sarah Jane Harrison, and Patrick Ryan Gallagher to be husband and wife. You may kiss the bride."

Once again there was laughter from the guests when Patrick and Sarah forgot they had an audience and the kiss continued until Father O'Shannahan had to clear his throat and remind the newly weds they still had to sign some papers.

The afternoon was wonderful. A Celtic quartet played traditional Irish music while people helped themselves to the feast Hannah had prepared.

The party continued long into the evening. Just before it was time for Patrick and Sarah to head off for their honeymoon she threw the bouquet. A dozen young women she didn't know all gathered on the lawn to catch the flowers. Sarah looked at them all before she turned her back to them and tossed the bouquet over her left shoulder. It must have been her imagination. For a second she swore she saw a girl with long red hair that looked exactly like Evelyn Elizabeth in the middle of the group. It must have been the setting sun in her eyes, she thought. For when she turned around there was no woman with red hair among those hoping to catch the bouquet.

Then Sarah and Patrick smiled and waved before they got into a limousine and drove away. As Hannah watched, she wiped a tear away and whispered "Well girlie this day you've waited so long to happen is almost over. Wasn't it a beautiful wedding?"

The garden air was sweet with the scent of wild flowers and there on the rock wall was a lady slipper.

"Yes, Padraig he is a lucky man indeed," Hannah said in a whisper.

Epilogue

Harrison House Inn opened its doors to guests one month after Patrick and Sarah had returned from their honeymoon. For the rest of the fall and throughout the winter months it became a popular place for business travelers. Many couples were booking their weddings to be held there. The inn was going to be very busy in tourist season.

Hannah was doing her best to teach Sarah how to cook, but Sarah said she was a hopeless case and told the older woman she could never leave them or Harrison House because they would be lost without her and the business would fail.

"Your delicious meals are the reason the inn is doing so well."

Hannah smiled. She always did love it when people praised her food.

"Yes, girl it's true. You would be lost without me. So I guess I have no choice but to stay."

By the first of May Sarah was very pregnant. As the days passed and she came closer to her due date, she became more uncomfortable and Patrick became more nervous.

Hannah tried to be a calming presence and did her best to reassure both of them that everything was going to be okay. She made all of Sarah's favorite foods and she insisted the young woman put her feet up and rest rather than clean and see to the guests needs.

"You are about to do the greatest job in the world and you need your energy. Now whatever needs doing around here, Patrick and I will take care of it," she told Sarah.

On April 10 at 3:35 a.m. Sarah woke Patrick up and told him that her water had broken and that it was time to go to the hospital. The baby arrived six hours later. Patrick held Sarah's hand throughout the delivery and when the baby took her first breath he looked into her eyes and declared she was the miniature version of her beautiful mother.

As Patrick and one of the labour-and-delivery nurses took the baby to weigh and measure her, the nurse asked Patrick what they'd decided to call her.

"This little lady is Evelyn Elizabeth Hannah Gallagher. Evie for short."

"That's a beautiful name for a beautiful baby," the nurse said.

"It comes from my wife's side of the family and a very dear friend who is like a second mother to us," Patrick explained.

When Hannah arrived at the hospital she found Sarah asleep in her bed and Patrick dozing in the chair beside her.

Hannah pulled the blankets up to Sarah's shoulders to be sure she didn't get a chill and then she found another blanket to place over Patrick. She decided not to wake them and quietly went to the nursery to meet the newest member of the family.

There in a bassinette was a wee little one with coppery red curls wrapped in a flannel blanket. Hannah smiled and waved to the sleepy baby.

"Welcome to the world Evie. You have a wonderful life ahead of you and your Auntie Hannah is going to spoil you rotten."

Standing over the bassinet was a woman with the same coppery shade of hair. She looked at Hannah and smiled. Hannah looked up to meet her gaze and tears filled her eyes.

"She is a true Harrison beauty with the same red hair as her mother and you. Isn't it wonderful they named the wee lass after you and I?"

The lights in the nursery seemed to take on a warm glow and all the babies hushed at once.

Ever so softly you could hear a deep warm male voice say: "This one shall be loved and watched over, from this moment and for always."

As Hannah placed her hand over her breast, she watched as not one, but two peaceful figures held hands and smiled into each other's eyes. The circle had been completed.

"Aye, and God Bless you both dear ones."

Haunted Heart / Laverne Stewart

About The Author:

Laverne Stewart, critically acclaimed best-selling author of non-fiction books *Angels and the Afterlife*, and, *Healing After Homicide – The Jackie Clark Story* (Manor House), has now produced a remarkable fiction offering – *Haunted Heart* (Manor House), a gripping novel of tragic romance and ghostly encounters.

Haunted Heart, the writer's first novel, was a natural progression for Laverne Stewart, who has been putting thoughts to paper as long as she's been able to hold a pencil. She knew in high school that a writing career was her life's ambition.

Laverne Stewart is also a 30-year journalism veteran. After a year as a radio news anchor she made the move to television. She spent 11 years with CTV as a news magazine investigative reporter before she made the leap to print journalism. She's an award-winning journalist and author. This is her third book.

When she's not writing about the gritty reality of life in this world she is making contact with those in the afterlife. Her first book, *Angels and the Afterlife*, opened the door to *Healing After Homicide*, and provided inspiration for *Haunted Heart*.

Laverne Stewart loves spending time with her husband, their two children, and the family's dog and cat at their lakeside New Brunswick home.

Haunted Heart / Laverne Stewart

Manor House
905-648-2193

www.ingramcontent.com/pod-product-compliance
Lightning Source LLC
Chambersburg PA
CBHW070054080526
44586CB00013B/1048